MACAT

An Analysis of

Eugene Genovese's

Roll, Jordan, Roll
The World the Slaves Made

Cheryl Hudson
with
Eva Namusoke

Published by Macat International Ltd
24:13 Coda Centre, 189 Munster Road, London SW6 6AW.

Distributed exclusively by Routledge
2 Park Square, Milton Park, Abingdon, Oxon OX14 4RN
711 Third Avenue, New York, NY 10017, USA

Routledge is an imprint of the Taylor & Francis Group, an informa business

Copyright © 2017 by Macat International Ltd
Macat International has asserted its right under the Copyright, Designs and Patents Act
1988 to be identified as the copyright holder of this work.

www.macat.com
info@macat.com

Cataloguing in Publication Data
A catalogue record for this book is available from the British Library.
Library of Congress Cataloguing-in-Publication Data is available upon request.
Cover illustration: Etienne Gilfillan

ISBN 978-1-912302-58-1 (hardback)
ISBN 978-1-912128-90-7 (paperback)
ISBN 978-1-912281-46-6 (e-book)

Notice

CONTENTS

THE MACAT LIBRARY

The Macat Library is a series of unique academic explorations of seminal works in the humanities and social sciences – books and papers that have had a significant and widely recognised impact on their disciplines. It has been created to serve as much more than just a summary of what lies between the covers of a great book. It illuminates and explores the influences on, ideas of, and impact of that book. Our goal is to offer a learning resource that encourages critical thinking and fosters a better, deeper understanding of important ideas.

Each publication is divided into three Sections: Influences, Ideas, and Impact. Each Section has four Modules. These explore every important facet of the work, and the responses to it.

This Section-Module structure makes a Macat Library book easy to use, but it has another important feature. Because each Macat book is written to the same format, it is possible (and encouraged!) to cross-reference multiple Macat books along the same lines of inquiry or research. This allows the reader to open up interesting interdisciplinary pathways.

To further aid your reading, lists of glossary terms and people mentioned are included at the end of this book (these are indicated by an asterisk [*] throughout) – as well as a list of works cited.

Macat has worked with the University of Cambridge to identify the elements of critical thinking and understand the ways in which six different skills combine to enable effective thinking.
Three allow us to fully understand a problem; three more give us the tools to solve it. Together, these six skills make up the **PACIER** model of critical thinking. They are:

ANALYSIS – understanding how an argument is built
EVALUATION – exploring the strengths and weaknesses of an argument
INTERPRETATION – understanding issues of meaning

CREATIVE THINKING – coming up with new ideas and fresh connections
PROBLEM-SOLVING – producing strong solutions
REASONING – creating strong arguments

To find out more, visit **WWW.MACAT.COM.**

CRITICAL THINKING AND *AND ROLL, JORDAN, ROLL*

Primary critical thinking skill: PROBLEM-SOLVING
Secondary critical thinking skill: REASONING

Most studies of slavery are underpinned by ideology and idealism. Eugene Genovese's ground-breaking book takes a stand against both these influences, arguing not only that all ideological history is bad history – a remarkable statement, coming from a self-professed Marxist – but also that slavery itself can only be understood if master and slave are studied together, rather than separately.

Genovese's most important insight, which makes this book a fine example of the critical thinking skill of problem-solving, is that the best way to view the institution of American slavery is to understand why exactly it was structured as it was. He saw slavery as a process of continual renegotiation of power balances, as masters strove to extract the maximum work from their slaves, while slaves aimed to obtain acknowledgement of their humanity and the ability to shape elements of the world that they were forced to live in.

Genovese's thesis is not wholly original; he adapts Gramsci's notion of hegemony to re-interpret the master-slave relationship – but it is an important example of the benefits of asking productive new questions about topics that seem, superficially at least, to be entirely obvious. By focusing on slave culture, rather than producing another study of economic determinism, this massive study succeeds in reconceptualising an institution in an exciting new way.

ABOUT THE AUTHOR OF THE ORIGINAL WORK

Eugene Genovese was an American historian whose ideas about American slavery sparked passionate debate. Born in 1930 in Brooklyn, New York, a teenage Genovese declared himself a Marxist and, writing during the Cold War as he did, his political beliefs were considered highly controversial. Nonetheless Genovese became a respected academic, interested in the power of ideas to make a difference. His belief that the cultural values of a group can help unravel their history is still influential today. Genovese died in 2012 at the age of 82.

ABOUT THE AUTHORS OF THE ANALYSIS

Dr Cheryl Hudson holds a PhD in history from Vanderbilt University, where her work examined the political culture of Chicago, 1890-1930. Currently a University Teacher in American history at the University of Liverpool, she has taught at universities in the UK and the USA, including Oxford, Sheffield, Coventry, Vanderbilt, Sussex and Kent, and is a former director of the academic programme at the Rothermere American Institute, University of Oxford.

Dr Eva Namusoke took her PhD in history from the University of Cambridge with work focusing on the history of the church in twentieth-century Uganda. She is currently a research fellow at the Institute of Commonwealth Studies, at the School of Advanced Study, University of London.

ABOUT MACAT

GREAT WORKS FOR CRITICAL THINKING

Macat is focused on making the ideas of the world's great thinkers accessible and comprehensible to everybody, everywhere, in ways that promote the development of enhanced critical thinking skills.

It works with leading academics from the world's top universities to produce new analyses that focus on the ideas and the impact of the most influential works ever written across a wide variety of academic disciplines. Each of the works that sit at the heart of its growing library is an enduring example of great thinking. But by setting them in context – and looking at the influences that shaped their authors, as well as the responses they provoked – Macat encourages readers to look at these classics and game-changers with fresh eyes. Readers learn to think, engage and challenge their ideas, rather than simply accepting them.

'Macat offers an amazing first-of-its-kind tool for interdisciplinary learning and research. Its focus on works that transformed their disciplines and its rigorous approach, drawing on the world's leading experts and educational institutions, opens up a world-class education to anyone.'

Andreas Schleicher
Director for Education and Skills, Organisation for Economic Co-operation and Development

'Macat is taking on some of the major challenges in university education ... They have drawn together a strong team of active academics who are producing teaching materials that are novel in the breadth of their approach.'

Prof Lord Broers,
former Vice-Chancellor of the University of Cambridge

'The Macat vision is exceptionally exciting. It focuses upon new modes of learning which analyse and explain seminal texts which have profoundly influenced world thinking and so social and economic development. It promotes the kind of critical thinking which is essential for any society and economy. This is the learning of the future.'

Rt Hon Charles Clarke, former UK Secretary of State for Education

'The Macat analyses provide immediate access to the criti~ conversation surrounding the books that have shape~ ~urce respective discipline, which will make them an inv~'~ld.' to all of those, students and teachers, work~ ~iego

Professor William Tronzo, University of C~

WAYS IN TO THE TEXT

KEY POINTS

- Eugene Genovese (1930–2012) was an American historian of the American South and American slavery.
- His book *Roll, Jordan, Roll* (1974) investigates the nature of the master–slave relationship in the US South from the founding of the nation until the Civil War.
- *Roll, Jordan, Roll* argues that the power of the slaveholders meant that their world view dominated society.

Who Was Eugene Genovese?

Eugene Dominick Genovese, the author of *Roll Jordan Roll: The World the Slaves Made* (1974), was born on May 19, 1930 in Brooklyn, New York. His father was an immigrant dockworker, and Eugene grew up in a working-class family in an ethnic Italian community. At the age of 15 he joined the Communist Party USA,* but he was expelled at the age of 20 for disregarding party discipline—or, as he said, he "zigged when [he] was supposed to zag."[1] He was later discharged from army service for his communist* leanings. Despite these experiences, Genovese remained a Marxist* thinker (that is, his historical analysis of society was founded on the work of the economist and social theorist Karl Marx*) until the 1980s.

He earned his bachelor's degree from Brooklyn College in 1953 and his PhD in 1959 from Columbia University, and went on to teach at more than a dozen universities, including Yale, Cambridge, and Rutgers. During a lecture at an antiwar event in 1965, at the height of the American war in Vietnam,* he caused controversy when he gave his support to the Vietcong,* the United States' opponents in the war, with the words: "I do not fear or regret the impending Vietcong victory in Vietnam. I welcome it."[2]

Although his words caused a scandal, Genovese's academic career survived. He published his greatest work, *Roll, Jordan, Roll* in 1974. But as the decades passed Genovese became increasingly frustrated by what he perceived to be the moralism (that is, the judgmental nature) of the American Left.* After gradually shifting away from Marxist ideology, Genovese and his wife, the historian Elizabeth Fox-Genovese,* both converted to conservative Catholicism, and Genovese rethought many of his earlier beliefs.

He died on September 26, 2012 at the age of 82. He is now regarded as a much admired but controversial historian and public intellectual.

What Does *Roll, Jordan, Roll* Say?

First published in 1974, *Roll, Jordan, Roll* is an epic 800-page study of the evolution of slavery in America over the course of the eighteenth and nineteenth centuries. Using extensive source material, including slave narratives (the testimony of slaves and former slaves), Genovese builds up a picture of the "world the slaves made."

He argues for a more complex understanding of the relationship between master and slaves, according to which slaves did not passively accept their role but, rather, engaged in a relationship defined both by resistance and by accommodation with their masters. In the process, slaves were able to assert their humanity and to challenge the institution of slavery. The book's subtitle is *The World the Slaves Made.* As this suggests, Genovese looks at ways in which slaves constructed their cultural world: creating song, prayers, and everyday forms of resistance. In doing so, slaves confirmed and maintained their humanity. They did so despite living within a system that dehumanized them and considered them property.

Genovese used the concept of paternalism*—a sort of institutionalized "parent–child" relationship, marked by an imbalance in status—to investigate slavery in the American South. An earlier historian, Ulrich Phillips,* had used this term to describe the attitude slaveholders had toward their slaves. For Phillips, it meant that slaveholders felt they had a parental duty to care for and discipline the "slaves, whom they regarded as primitive." Both slaveholders and slaves had duties and responsibilities toward one another.

For Phillips, paternalism was benevolent in nature. But Genovese's interpretation is different. If the slaveholders saw themselves as benevolent, he argues, the slaves did not see them in that way; paternalism forced slaveholders to see their slaves as humans, not just as movable property—which gave slaves a way of challenging their power. The slave-labor system as a whole, Genovese concludes, indicates the precapitalist* status of the Southern United States.

This text remains a landmark in the study of American slavery because of its focus on the agency (or power) of slaves. Genovese's concept of paternalism allowed for a new understanding of slavery to develop. *Roll, Jordan, Roll* thus helped to reinvigorate the field of slavery studies.

Genovese's study of slavery was quite unorthodox. He followed the Italian neo-Marxist political theorist Antonio Gramsci,* who had rejected Marx's concept of "economic determinism"* by challenging the idea that economic structure is the key organizing force in society. Like Gramsci, Genovese emphasized instead the role of culture. Genovese argued that cultural forms—hymns or dances, for example—served as weapons of both oppression and liberation. For him, neither slave nor master was morally "good" or "bad." His refusal to make moral judgments made his book highly controversial.

The book covers many aspects of slave life, from religion to resistance, but does not ignore the slaveholder. This is why historians consider *Roll, Jordan, Roll* both groundbreaking and comprehensive. It sits alongside classic works such as the historian Kenneth Stampp's* *The Peculiar Institution* (1956) to produce a major reinterpretation of the study of slavery.

Roll, Jordan, Roll won the Anisfield-Wolf Book Award and the prestigious Bancroft Prize for American history. The book retains a place on university syllabi. Its scholarship is widely admired even if its theoretical approach is no longer emulated.

Why Does *Roll, Jordan, Roll* Matter?

Roll, Jordan, Roll was published at a time of renewed interest in the study of slavery. The American civil rights movement* of the 1950s and 1960s, which called for equal legal and political rights for African Americans, had brought this group onto the national and international stage. Scholars became keen to reexamine the experience of black Americans throughout US history. In particular, they began to reexamine the horrors black slaves endured during slavery.

Since *Roll, Jordan, Roll* was published, however, both scholarship and racial politics have moved on. African American and feminist historians have disputed and criticized aspects of Genovese's book. It is sometimes charged with displaying the very racism it sought to challenge. Yet, the book represented a radically new way of looking at the subject of slavery and retains much that is still of value. It insists that the institution of slavery cannot be fully understood by looking at slaves in isolation. They must be placed in relation to the slave owner.

The late eighteenth-century and early nineteenth-century German philosopher G. W. F. Hegel* had developed the notion of the master–slave dialectic,* or dialogue. In this dialectic, interactions between two opposing forces have an impact on both of the forces. By placing the master–slave relationship at the center of his analysis, Genovese adopts a Hegelian* framework for *Roll, Jordan, Roll.* Continuing debates about race and cultural identity in both academic and public circles attest to the relevance of his work.

If *Roll, Jordan, Roll* remains a crucial text in slavery studies decades after its publication this is due in part to the extensive source material it presents. Genovese accessed and examined a mass of archival material over ten years of research—a feat that historians of slavery are unlikely to reproduce. As a result, all serious scholars of slavery must at some point engage with Genovese's work.

Genovese also presents a compelling, if controversial, understanding of slavery. The American historian Peter Kolchin* calls Genovese our "greatest historian of slavery."[3] Another American historian, Steven Hahn,* describes *Roll, Jordan, Roll* as "the finest work on slavery ever produced."[4] Even scholars who disagree with Genovese's theoretical framework must still engage with his text. The sheer depth of original material Genovese examined and the innovative and compelling analysis he provided make this unavoidable.

NOTES

1 Douglas Martin, "Eugene D. Genovese, Historian of South, Dies at 82," *New York Times,* September 29, 2012, http://www.nytimes.com/2012/09/30/us/eugene-d-genovese-historian-of-south-dies-at-82.html?_r=0, accessed June 25, 2015.

2 Martin, "Eugene D. Genovese."

3 Peter Kolchin, "Eugene D. Genovese: Historian of Slavery," *Radical History Review* 88 (Winter 2004): 64.

4 Steven Hahn, "From Radical to Right-Wing: The Legacy of Eugene Genovese," *The New Republic,* October 2, 2012, http://www.newrepublic.com/article/books-and-arts/108044/radical-right-wing-the-legacy-eugene-genovese, accessed June 30, 2015.

SECTION 1
INFLUENCES

MODULE 1
THE AUTHOR AND THE HISTORICAL CONTEXT

KEY POINTS

- *Roll, Jordan, Roll* remains relevant for the breadth of its research and the clarity of its argument.

- Eugene Genovese was a Marxist* thinker, following the analysis of society proposed by the economist and political theorist Karl Marx. He hoped his ideas would have an impact both inside and outside academic circles.

- Genovese was writing at the time of the Cold War (a period of tension between the capitalist* United States and the communist* Soviet Union, together with nations aligned to each) and the civil rights movement* in America. He also witnessed the rise of the New Left,* a political movement calling for a broad range of reforms, in areas including gay rights, gender roles, and drug laws.

Why Read This Text?

Eugene D. Genovese's book *Roll, Jordan, Roll: The World the Slaves Made* was published in 1974 and remains one of the most important books written about American slavery. It focuses on the period between the late eighteenth century and the American Civil War of 1861–65*—a war fought between the forces of the Republican North and the Confederate South, after which slaves in the US were officially given their freedom. Its aim was to provide an analysis of slavery in the United States.

Genovese places the Marxist idea of class struggle at the heart of his book, looking closely at the relationship between master and slave in

> ❝ Eugene Genovese's scholarship made an enormous difference despite the challenges that he faced. As a self-proclaimed Marxist, he had to make his way through an unreceptive professional discipline–history–in a country still feeling the effects of McCarthyism, and he took on one of the central areas of historical interpretation, the coming and significance of the Civil War. ❞
>
> Steven Hahn, "From Radical to Right Wing"

the antebellum* ("pre-war") South. While the work is impressive for its historical and geographical scope, it is Genovese's focus on this relationship that serves to distinguish it from other studies. Other historians have looked at the slaves' experience alone, dismissing the motives and actions of the slaveholders as "evil," but Genovese takes the slaveholders seriously. His inclusion of them in the political, social, and cultural dynamics of the institution of slavery made an important impact on the field.

Specifically, Genovese introduces the concept of paternalism*—a sort of institutionalized "parent–child" relationship, marked by an imbalance in status—as a distinct and defining feature of the American master–slave dynamic. Paternalism often limits the autonomy, or independence, of an individual or group. Genovese argues that adopting a paternalistic attitude to justify their rule forced slaveholders to recognize the humanity of slaves, but also allowed oppression to take place. Genovese reveals the subtle ways in which slaves tried to resist this, and describes their acts of day-to-day resistance, such as working slowly or committing acts of vandalism as, at best, a "prepolitical" accommodation and, at worst, "pathetic nihilism [negativity]."[1] But he shows that slaves did create an autonomous culture that allowed them to assert their own humanity.

Genovese's discussion of this dynamic class relationship has meant that *Roll, Jordan, Roll* has remained a landmark in the study of American slavery.

Author's Life

Genovese was a second-generation Italian immigrant, the son of a dockworker father and homemaker mother. He was born in 1930 in Brooklyn, New York. As an idealistic youth, he joined the Communist Party USA—a political party of like-minded Marxists—and remained a member for five years. Although the party revoked his membership for not following the party line, Genovese was later discharged from the US Army because of his communist background. Marxism continued to influence his thinking at least until the 1980s.[2]

Genovese earned his undergraduate degree at Brooklyn College in 1953. He went on to take advanced graduate degrees at Columbia University, receiving his PhD in 1959. He taught at more than a dozen colleges, including Yale University, the University of Cambridge, and Rutgers University. At Rutgers in 1965, comments he made about the Vietnam War* caused great controversy. At an antiwar event he announced in the course of a lecture: "I do not fear or regret the impending Vietcong victory in Vietnam. I welcome it."[3] It is worth noting, however, that in 1969 he argued against the American Historical Association adopting an antiwar position, since this would alienate those who supported the war.

The years he spent at the University of Rochester between 1969 and 1986 would prove the most productive years of Genovese's life. But, rejecting what he perceived to be the dogmatic moralism of the academic Left, in the 1990s he shifted away from Marxism and converted to conservative Catholicism. This shift, too, brought controversy. Genovese began arguing for religious instruction in schools and opposing access to abortion and special laws to protect homosexuals. After spending the final years of his career teaching in a handful of colleges and universities in the US South, Genovese died in September 2012, aged 82.[4]

Author's Background

The Cold War was at its height when Eugene Genovese was writing and publishing his most important works. An American Marxist, he had grown up in the radical 1930s, when the Communist Party USA was an active part of the American Left,* and came to maturity during the 1950s during the McCarthy* era, when anti-communist "witch-hunts" led by Senator Joe McCarthy made life and work very difficult for Americans suspected of having communist sympathies. Genovese used Marxism's analytical tools to explore the American past, examining the relationships of power and inequality in the antebellum South—that is, the Southern states before the Civil War. He argued that the institution of slavery as it existed in the United States was "precapitalist."*

Capitalism is the dominant social and economic system in the West, and increasingly throughout the developing world. For Genovese, the cultural values of the Southern states, both positive and negative, were destroyed by it.

The 1950s also saw the civil rights movement gain momentum. There were widespread campaigns throughout the South tackling racial discrimination and calling for civil rights* for African Americans. Both African American and white scholars were then rejecting and revising earlier historical accounts of slavery as a "civilizing" force, and the political climate drove historians in the 1960s and 1970s to produce more nuanced, or subtle, studies of slavery. Genovese's work, however, unlike that of his contemporaries, played down the role of racism in perpetuating slavery. He refused to adopt a simple moral position that condemned slaveholders. Instead, he tried to understand their motivations and actions. This led to conflict with historians and others from the New Left, and the conflict continued throughout his career.

In the 1990s, Genovese came to directly challenge the political positions held by the New Left and became a conservative Catholic.

NOTES

1   Eugene Genovese, *Roll, Jordan, Roll: The World the Slaves Made* (New York: Vintage Books, 1976), 598, 659.

2   Elaine Woo, "Eugene Genovese Dies at 82; Leftist Historian Turned Conservative," *Los Angeles Times*, October 15, 2012, http://articles. latimes.com/2012/oct/15/local/la-me-eugene-genovese-20121015, accessed June 29, 2015; Douglas Martin, "Eugene D. Genovese, Historian of South, Dies at 82," *New York Times,* September 29, 2012, http://www. nytimes.com/2012/09/30/us/eugene-d-genovese-historian-of-south-dies-at-82.html, accessed June 25, 2015.

3   Woo, "Eugene Genovese Dies"; Martin, "Eugene D. Genovese."

4   Martin, "Eugene D. Genovese."

ACADEMIC CONTEXT

KEY POINTS

- Those studying the historical field of US slavery were concerned with the nature of the "peculiar institution" — a euphemism for slavery in the American South.

- Very little had been written on the history of slavery before the 1960s, but the work of the historian Ulrich Phillips* — whose analysis of slavery was often viewed as a racist justification of the institution — dominated the field.

- Eugene Genovese's work paid homage to previous scholarship, including that of Phillips, but Genovese challenged most prior assumptions about plantation life and slave culture. He helped to reinvigorate the study of slavery.

The Work in its Context

Eugene Genovese published *Roll, Jordan, Roll: The World the Slaves Made* at a time when interest in African American history was rising. When the field of slavery studies first emerged in the early part of the twentieth century, historians had been interested in understanding slavery as an economic and political institution and as a cause of the American Civil War.* They had asked whether the existence of slavery had made the war itself inevitable. The field's founding scholar, the American historian Ulrich B. Phillips, however, argued that the war had not been inevitable, and it had also been unnecessary.

Although slavery was abolished throughout the United States after the Northern states won the Civil War, Phillips believed that slavery's structural weaknesses meant that it would have come to an end anyway. Genovese had written about the economics of slavery in the

> ❝ Although Genovese's most important contribution
> has been as a historian of slavery, he has also had a major
> impact on the historical profession—and on academia
> in general—as an outspoken Marxist. Being a radical
> professor may not seem especially noteworthy today, but
> it was in the 'liberal' 1960s, when professing left-wing
> views was enough to put one's career in jeopardy. ...
> As much as any other one individual, I think, Genovese
> helped change this situation, making it possible for
> an outspoken radical to enter the mainstream of the
> American historical profession. ❞
>
> Peter Kolchin, "Eugene D. Genovese: Historian of Slavery"

1960s, when that was still an active field of research.¹ In the post-World War II* period, however, and especially following the 1960s civil rights movement,* historians' interests, including those of Genovese, began to shift toward the impact of slavery on slaves themselves. While Ulrich Phillips had suggested that slavery was broadly beneficial and the treatment of slaves broadly benign, historians in the 1950s and 1960s challenged this position. They set out to demonstrate the ways in which slavery was detrimental to slaves' lives, culture, and experiences.

Overview of the Field

In the early part of the twentieth century, Ulrich Phillips published two key books that broadly defined the field of American slavery studies. In *American Negro Slavery* (written in 1918) and *Life and Labor in the Old South* (1929), he set out three major propositions. First, he argued that the plantation system was structurally weak and economically unviable. He believed it would have faded away even without the Civil War. Second, Phillips noted that slaveholders' treatment of slaves was benevolent and that slavery worked to civilize, educate, and Christianize "primitive" Africans. Finally, he argued that race, especially white supremacy, was the "central theme of Southern history."[2]

Historians now dismiss much of Phillips's writing as racist and view him as an apologist for slavery. Two American historians—Herbert Aptheker in his book *American Negro Slave Revolts* (1943) and Stanley Elkins in his book *Slavery* (1959)—offer direct challenges to Phillips's claims. Both Aptheker and Elkins argue that slaves were treated badly, though they differed in the way they believed slaves reacted to the bad treatment. While Aptheker drew attention to rebellious slave revolts, Elkins, comparing plantations to Nazi* concentration camps in their psychological effects, suggests that slavery created lazy, dishonest, and child-like personalities among slaves.

Other scholars also believe that slaves endured terrible treatment rather than enjoying the benevolence Phillips describes. In *The Peculiar Institution* (1956), the American historian Kenneth Stampp* strongly rejects Phillips's account of slavery.[3] Genovese himself, in the foreword to the 1966 edition of Phillips's *American Negro Slavery*, referred to the historian as "a racist, however benign and paternalistic."*[4] Eight years later, Genovese's own book, *Roll, Jordan, Roll*, proposed distinct ideas about how slavery was experienced by both slaves and masters. It also examined why slave rebellions were relatively infrequent in America.[5]

Academic Influences

Genovese's primary concern in *Roll, Jordan, Roll* was the nature of the master–slave relationship and the "world the slaves made." He sought to salvage the valuable elements of Phillips's thinking, such as his recognition of the weak economic structure of slavery. But Genovese also wanted to explore the actions and agency of the slaves themselves. Many of Phillips's critics had simply listed atrocities against slaves instead of the kindnesses Phillips had described. But as the American historians George Frederickson* and Christopher Lasch* note:"Both methods suffer from the same defect: they attempt to solve a conceptual problem—what did slavery do to the slave?—by accumulating quantitative evidence … The only conclusion that one can legitimately draw from this debate is that great variations in treatment existed from plantation to plantation."[6]

Rather than asking what slavery did to the slave, Genovese asks what the slaves did for themselves. In *Roll, Jordan, Roll* he suggests that slaves created a culture that opposed slavery. Through their families, communities, and religion, slaves cultivated a measure of human dignity and autonomy. Genovese adapts Phillips's concept of paternalism, transforming it into a cultural critique of slavery. Rather than benign benevolence, he argues that slaves experienced planter paternalism as largely, if not entirely, oppressive.

Outside his immediate field, Genovese's greatest influence was the Italian Marxist cultural critic Antonio Gramsci*—notably for his concept of cultural hegemony,* or domination, which explained how the world view of the ruling class came to be shared by other social groups, reinforcing domination by the elite. Genovese argues that slaveholders used paternalism (backed by the threat of violence) to assert dominance.[7]

The pioneering British social historian E. P. Thompson* also influenced Genovese's understanding of class, culture, and historical change.[8] Both Gramsci and Thompson rejected classic Marxist economic determinism* (the belief that economic systems, above all, determine social outcomes), looking instead to cultural ideas to understand class conflict.

NOTES

1   Eugene Genovese, *The Political Economy of Slavery: Studies in the Economy and the Society of the Slave South* (New York: Vintage Books, 1965).

2   Ulrich B. Phillips, "The Central Theme of Southern History," *American Historical Review* 34, no. 1 (1928): 30–43.

3   Kenneth Stampp, *The Peculiar Institution: Slavery in the Antebellum South* (New York: Knopf, 1956).

4   Eugene Genovese, "Foreword," in Ulrich Bonnell Phillips, *American Negro Slavery: A Survey of the Supply, Employment and Control of Negro Labor as Determined by the Plantation Regime* (Baton Rouge: Louisiana State University Press, 1966 [new edition, with a new foreword]).

5   Manisha Sinha, "Eugene D. Genovese: The Mind of a Marxist Conservative," *Radical History Review* 88 (Winter 2004): 8.

6   George Fredrickson and Christopher Lasch, "Resistance to Slavery," *Civil War History* 13 (1967): 316.

7   Eugene D. Genovese, *Roll, Jordan, Roll: The World the Slaves Made* (New York: Vintage Books, 1976): 26–7.

8   E. P. Thompson, *The Making of the English Working Class* (London: Victor Gollancz, 1963).

THE PROBLEM

KEY POINTS

- In 1974, when *Roll, Jordan, Roll* was published, historians of slavery were debating what impact the experience of slavery had on the outlook, personality, and life experience of slaves.

- The American historian Ulrich B. Phillips* had characterized slaves as mostly well cared for and content, and in fact benefiting from the experience of slavery in many ways. Revisionist* historians (historians reinterpreting orthodox understandings), however, responded by revealing the legal, social, cultural, and psychological harm caused by slavery.

- Eugene Genovese took Phillips's claims about the intentions of the slaveholders seriously. While Genovese accepts that slavery caused great harm, he focuses on slaves as actors in the historical drama of slavery. They acted, as well as being acted upon.

Core Question

Eugene Genovese's *Roll, Jordan, Roll: The World the Slaves Made* pays attention both to what slaves did and to what was done to them. Against the backdrop of the civil rights movement* of the 1950s and 1960s, in which Americans of African ancestry organized to fight racial inequality and claim their social and political rights, historians were encouraged to explore how African slaves had responded to the experience of slavery. Justifications for slavery made by white Southerners also became a matter of interest in historical research.

> ❝ Southern paternalism, like every other paternalism, had little to do with Ole Massa's ostensible benevolence, kindness and good cheer. It grew out of the necessity to discipline and morally justify a system of exploitation. It did encourage kindness and affection, but it simultaneously encouraged cruelty and hatred. The racial distinction between master and slave heightened the tension inherent in an unjust social order. ❞
> *Eugene Genovese,* Roll, Jordan, Roll

Revisionist historians dismissed the pioneering historian of American slavery, Ulrich B. Phillips,* as a racist apologist for slavery.[1] Phillips had argued that slaveholders had a paternalistic affection for their slaves and felt they had a duty to educate, Christianize, and uplift them. Revisionists point out that if slavery was a benevolent school, it was one that no slaves ever graduated from. American historians such as Stanley Elkins* and Kenneth Stampp* argue that far from "civilizing" slaves, slavery damaged their psychological health, contorted and stifled the development of their personalities, stripped them of their African culture, and prevented them from participating in American culture.

Genovese rescued Phillips's concept of paternalism* from this far-reaching revisionism by presenting slavery as an institution in which slaves both accepted and resisted their lot in life. Although slaves had little recourse to legal or political escape, he argued, they found ways to carve out cultural autonomy and resistance to their masters' power. In Genovese's interpretation, slaveholders did view slaves as property but were also paternalistic toward them. This paternalism grew from the psychological contortions slaveholders went through in order to justify the institution of slavery, and forced them to recognize that slaves were human. Genovese presented slavery as a conflict between classes. He reoriented the debate by asking what impact slaves themselves had on the institution of slavery.

The Participants

In his book *American Negro Slavery* (written in 1918), Phillips addresses the question of how slaves experienced slavery and the impact this had. "Every plantation of the standard Southern type," he argues, "was, in fact, a school constantly training and controlling pupils who were in a backward state of civilization."[2]

In responding to this, historians questioned Philips's sampling technique, pointing out that slavery regimes differed radically from plantation to plantation. The American Marxist historian Herbert Aptheker* also challenged Phillips's depiction of slavery as beneficial for slaves, noting that slaves gained nothing from slavery apart from a desire for freedom. He stated that this was a truth that could no longer be ignored:

"Contemporary evidence of newspapers, court records, journals, diaries, letters, speeches makes crystal clear to anyone who views black men as human beings that American Negro slavery was a monstrously cruel system of exploitation and that its victims despised it and sought in every way possible to oppose it."[3]

Other scholars followed Aptheker's lead. In his book *The Peculiar Institution* (1959), the American historian Kenneth Stampp disputes Phillips's characterization of slavery, pointing out that slaves actively resisted their cruel treatment and conditions, not just through armed uprisings but also through work slowdowns, breaking tools, theft, and so on. In another book of 1959, *Slavery*, the American historian Stanley Elkins suggests that the harsh exploitation of slavery produced child-like compliance among slaves. Comparing plantations to Nazi* concentration camps, Elkins painted a portrayal of the "sambo" personality that slaves adopted to survive the system; "sambo" remains a word with very negative connotations today.

By the 1960s, most historians in the field had accepted that slavery was a negative experience for slaves, and debate moved on to the question of how they responded to the system—as passive victims or as defiant rebels?

The Contemporary Debate

Uncomfortable with the wholesale revision of Phillips's analysis, Genovese entered the debate with *Roll, Jordan, Roll*.

A new edition of *American Negro Slavery* was published in 1966, 32 years after Phillips's death. Genovese wrote the foreword, both acknowledging Phillips's racism and paying homage to his painstaking research and erudite scholarship. He states:

"Phillips came close to greatness as a historian, perhaps as close as any historian this country has produced. We may leave to those who live in the world of absolute good and evil the task of explaining how a man with such primitive views of fundamental social questions could write such splendid history."

Genovese argues that Phillips's historical analysis must be taken seriously. His foreword concludes that "*American Negro Slavery* is not the last word on its subject; merely the indispensable first."[4]

Although Genovese salvaged from Phillips the concept of paternalism,* he did not, however, adopt it wholesale. For Phillips, paternalism was benevolent in nature. Genovese, in contrast, noted that paternalism was sustained by violence and coercion. Like his contemporaries, Genovese was interested in looking for ways in which slaves shaped their own worlds. But his approach was unique, in that he explored the lives of slaves in the context of their social relationships—the most central of which was with their masters.

Slaves did not understand the relationship in the same way as the masters did, however. Nor did this relationship mean that slaves' relationships with one another were unimportant. *Roll, Jordan, Roll* examines slaves' families, communities, and cultural forms closely to outline the autonomous—that is, independent—spaces of resistance created by slaves. Finally, unlike other historians studying slavery, Genovese places Christianity at the heart of antebellum* plantation life.

NOTES

1   John David Smith, "The Life and Labor of Ulrich Bonnell Phillips," *Georgia Historical Quarterly* 70, no. 2 (Summer 1986): 257–8.

2   Ulrich B. Phillips, *American Negro Slavery* (New York: D. Appleton & Co.,1918), 342.

3   Herbert Aptheker, *American Negro Slave Revolts* (New York: International Publishers, 1943, reprint 1974), 2–3.

4   Eugene Genovese, "Foreword," in Ulrich Bonnell Phillips, *American Negro Slavery: A Survey of the Supply, Employment and Control of Negro Labor as Determined by the Plantation Regime* (Baton Rouge: Louisiana State University Press, 1966), vii.

THE AUTHOR'S CONTRIBUTION

KEY POINTS

- Eugene Genovese insisted that the nature of slavery could only be understood if both master and slave were studied in relation to one another.

- He argued that slavery represented a continual renegotiation of cultural power and position.

- Genovese's contribution to the study of slavery and the American South was immense. He provided a thorough and comprehensive response to the one-sidedness of both the American historian Ulrich B. Phillips* and Phillips's critics.

Author's Aims

In *Roll Jordan, Roll: The World the Slaves Made*, Eugene Genovese avoids a moralistic interpretation of the institution of slavery. Many of his contemporaries in the field of slavery studies were criticizing the scholarship of the American historian Ulrich B. Phillips by dismissing him as a racist. Genovese, while acknowledging Phillips's racism and bias, warns against developing an alternative historical understanding driven by a different ideology. Good history, Genovese urged, should be located in the empirical evidence (that is, in the evidence which can actually be observed and measured). All "ideologically motivated history," he wrote, "is bad history."[1]

In his own work, Genovese aimed to assimilate insights both from the work of Phillips and from that of the revisionists* (those historians questioning the old orthodoxy). He did so by developing a new theoretical model based on the concept of cultural hegemony* developed by the Italian Marxist cultural critic Antonio Gramsci.*

> ❝ The harsh truth is that racists like Phillips, until recently, have taught us much more about the South, and the Southern black man too, than their Northern liberal detractors have ever been able to do. I am sorry about that. It is terribly annoying. But there is not much to be done about it. ❞
>
> Eugene Genovese, *In Red and Black*

Cultural hegemony is the process by which the ideas of a ruling elite come to be adopted more widely throughout society. Social acceptance of these ideas reinforces the power of the elite. Genovese argues that the idea of paternalism* allowed the planters to assert and maintain their dominance. At the same time, this paternalism forced masters to acknowledge the humanity of their slaves. While revisionist historians sometimes portrayed slaves as powerless victims, Genovese shows instead that slaves moved between accommodating their treatment and resisting it.

Roll, Jordan, Roll is a masterpiece of empirical research, theoretical application, and historical analysis; it achieved and exceeded the goals Genovese set for it. The American historian Bertram Wyatt-Brown* calls it "an inspired repudiation of all the facile moral judgments that have scarred so many works about American racial history and practice."[2]

Approach

Genovese adapted Phillips's understanding of the master–slave relationship by combining the concept of paternalism with an analysis that also took account of the slaves' own struggle for autonomy and control. Unlike other revisionist scholars, Genovese did not focus solely on the lives and experiences of the slave community, but saw slavery as a continually renegotiated power relationship between master and slave. This, Genovese insists, is the only way to understand slavery objectively.

The book's subtitle, *The World the Slaves Made*, indicates that *Roll, Jordan, Roll* provides detailed descriptions of slaves' lives on Southern plantations. Genovese explores family life, wedding ceremonies, funerals, work habits, worship, and resistance, taking account of all the areas that gave the lives of slaves meaning. But he continually reminds the reader that these lives were lived inside the so-called "peculiar institution" of slavery.

Slaves found ways to express their humanity within a situation that dehumanized them. It was a constant contradictory struggle.

Genovese explains his theoretical framework in the opening section of the book. He emphasizes the dialectical* power struggle between slave and master, according to which both are changed through the resolution of oppositions in conflict. But instead of the economic determinism* of Marxism (that is, roughly, the idea that the economic system is paramount in deciding the structure and nature of a society), Genovese embraces a cultural interpretation of slavery. Although he agrees with other revisionists that more emphasis must be placed on the ability of slaves to shape their own world, he also points out the horrendous constraints under which slaves lived. His major contribution is to explore the world view of both master and slave and to highlight the many paradoxes within their relationship.

Contribution in Context

Both Genovese's arguments in *Roll, Jordan, Roll* and his methodological approach were highly innovative. Genovese uses the idea of paternalism to explain how slaveholders asserted and maintained their cultural hegemony (dominance) in the South as it existed in the years before the American Civil War.* He derived this concept from the work of the pioneering historian of slavery, Ulrich Phillips.

Although historians understood Phillips as seeking to justify the actions of slaveholders through his description of their paternalism, Genovese saw the concept of paternalism as a valuable tool nonetheless. In his hands, the idea gained complexity and depth. Paternalism to him did not simply denote kindness or imply that slavery was benign; for Genovese, paternalism "necessarily involves harshness and may even involve cruelty so long as it is within the context of a strong sense of duty and responsibility toward those in dependent status."[3] Phillips's conception of paternalism informs Genovese's work—but Genovese alters its meaning and use.

Genovese also revised and adapted the Marxist analysis that British historian E. P. Thompson* had pioneered in his masterful book of 1963, *The Making of the English Working Class*. Like Thompson, Genovese's methodological approach involved building a cultural history from "the bottom up" (that is, by beginning his analysis through a consideration of people of low social status). Thompson allowed the industrial working class in Britain to speak through the sources, rather than through a theoretical imposition. Genovese did the same with plantation life. Gramsci's theory of cultural hegemony influenced both Thompson and Genovese; both historians use the theory in conjunction with empirical evidence.

NOTES

1   Eugene D. Genovese, "On Being a Socialist and a Historian," in *In Red and Black: Marxian Explorations in Southern and Afro-American History* (New York: Vintage Books, 1971), 4.

2   Bertram Wyatt-Brown, "*Roll, Jordan Roll: The World the Slaves Made*, by Eugene D. Genovese," *Journal of Southern History* 41, no. 2 (May 1975): 240–2.

3   Eugene Genovese, *Roll, Jordan, Roll: The World the Slaves Made* (New York: Vintage Books, 1976): 4–5.

SECTION 2
IDEAS

MAIN IDEAS

KEY POINTS

- The key theme of *Roll, Jordan, Roll* is the dialectical*
  relationship between master and slave in the antebellum*
  American South. The term "dialectical" refers, roughly, to
  a process of shared transformation through conflict, and
  Genovese uses it to describe the way the relationship of the
  master class and slave classes changed through confrontation.

- Genovese argues that the master–slave relationship was
  contradictory and ambiguous. It contained elements of
  repression and violence as well as elements of affection and
  liberation.

- Although Genovese uses Marxist* categories of analysis, he
  rejects Marx's idea that it is economies, first and foremost,
  that decide what a society will be like for those who make
  up its different classes. Instead, Genovese's focus is on the
  cultural power struggle between slaves and their masters.

Key Themes

The key theme of Eugene Genovese's *Roll, Jordan, Roll: The World the Slaves Made* is the master–slave relationship.

Genovese explores the many ways in which these two opposing classes influenced one another. For Genovese, slavery could not be understood by studying slaves or slaveholders alone: their relationship with each other is the important element. It was a relationship that contained conflict, power, familiarity, cooperation, violence, affection, and a great deal of contradiction and ambiguity.

Although Genovese's text covers the years in which capitalism*

> ❝ Paternalism and slavery merged into a single idea
> to the masters. But the slaves proved much more astute
> in separating the two; they acted consciously and
> unconsciously to transform paternalism into a doctrine
> of protection of their own rights—a doctrine that
> represented the negation of the idea of slavery itself. ❞
>
> Eugene Genovese, *Roll, Jordan, Roll*

was the dominant political and economic system in the West, as it still is, he argues that slavery did not in any way resemble a capital–labor relationship (according to which those who do the work do not own the tools and resources; these belong, instead, to the people who invested capital in the business and who make all the profits). He concludes that slavery in the antebellum South was precapitalist* in nature.

A second important theme of Genovese's text is the concept of paternalism.* Slaveholders believed that slaves were "primitive" and benefited from their contact with "benevolent" slaveholders through a relationship resembling that between parents and children.

Genovese argues that planters developed this outlook to ease the psychological conflict they experienced as a result of owning humans as property. Paternalism made an unequal and exploitative relationship appear mutually beneficial. Since both parties have duties to the other and experience living in close quarters, a seemingly close bond develops. Although this world view was not shared by slaves, planters were powerful enough to make their vision dominant. Genovese argues that the absence of large-scale rebellion among American slaves was partly the result of paternalism. But he emphasizes that it was mostly the result of differential power relations and the ever-present threat of violence.

The third central theme of the book looks at the master–slave relationship from the slave's perspective. Genovese believes that slaves redefined the meaning of paternalism, stressing the interdependence of the two classes rather than the benevolence of the slaveholders, and developing forms of cultural resistance to slavery. Religious faith and spirituality allowed slaves to assert their humanity and speak of their desire for freedom. Despite the relative absence of outright revolt, this cultural space let slaves exist with dignity, avoiding being dehumanized by their experience.

Exploring the Ideas

For Genovese, the key to understanding how slaves survived slavery and how slaveholders justified slavery lies in the relationship between these classes. He says a contradictory form of paternalism that was unique to the American South sustained the "peculiar institution": "[Paternalism] grew out of the necessity to discipline and morally justify a system of exploitation. It did encourage kindness and affection, but it simultaneously encouraged cruelty and hatred."[1]

In this system slaves must rely on their masters for protection despite being subject to their arbitrary discipline and exercise of power. And while slaveholders relied on their slaves for labor, living in close proximity meant they were forced to see them as human, not just as property. Paternalism therefore "gave the masters an interest in the preservation of the blacks and created a bond of human sympathy that led to an interest in their happiness as well."[2] Locked in a relationship that each class understood differently, slaves and slaveholders continually negotiated the extent and nature of their duties and responsibilities to the other.

Slaves understood that planters had a need to feel that their slaves were grateful to them. As a result they often accommodated their paternalism in order to negotiate limits on the power of the slaveholders; this helped slaves control the pace of work or receive recognition for their marriages, for example. Accommodating paternalism, then, both reinforced the slaves' position and aided their resistance. Reinterpreting paternalism as interdependence, slaves gained "a sense of moral worth." Alongside acceptance of their duties, they asserted their rights; "the slaves transformed their acquiescence in paternalism into a rejection of slavery itself."[3]

Yet, ultimately, Genovese argues that paternalism as a cultural ideal helped the planters maintain hegemonic (dominant) control over their workforce and society.

Language and Expression

Roll Jordan Roll is divided into four books, each with two parts:

- In Book One, Genovese explains the theoretical tools he will use to discuss slavery. The concept of paternalism is explained at the beginning of this book. He moves on to discuss the Italian cultural critic Antonio Gramsci's* concept of cultural hegemony,* exploring how slaveholders maintained their hold over their society through cultural means. These two concepts—paternalism and cultural hegemony—are applied to the study of slavery in an innovative and illuminating way.

- Book Two focuses on the contradictory role of Christianity in the lives of slaves and slaveholders. Slaves blended Christian and African traditions, transforming Christianity into a religion of resistance—"not often of revolutionary defiance, but of a spiritual resistance that accepted the limits of the politically possible."[4]

- Book Three utilizes and interprets a massive amount of primary source material as it explores the everyday lives of slaves.

- Book Four focuses on the ways in which slaves carved out spaces of dignity, resistance, and emancipation (that is, liberation).

Genovese's approach is forcefully interpretive and argumentative. This is no dry, factual account. His writing is passionate and engaged, and, despite his obvious ideological commitments, it remains accessible to undergraduate students and the educated lay public—even if the book's length, standing at over 800 pages, may deter some readers.

NOTES

1   Eugene D. Genovese, *Roll, Jordan, Roll: The World the Slaves Made* (New York: Vintage Books, 1976), 4.

2   Genovese, *Roll, Jordan, Roll*, 85.

3   Genovese, *Roll, Jordan, Roll*, 658.

4   Genovese, *Roll, Jordan, Roll*, 254.

MODULE 6
SECONDARY IDEAS

KEY POINTS

- There are two supporting ideas that both illustrate and add depth to Genovese's central argument: the issue of race and that of religion. Two other themes provide a foundation for his main thesis: the peculiarity of Southern slavery compared with the international experience, and the question of slavery's relation to capitalism.*

- These four secondary ideas had different impacts: the question of race provoked criticism and dissent; the question of religion encouraged deeper research; and both contextual questions joined larger debates that already had their own audiences.

- The role of religion in slavery might be judged the most important of these ideas since it was an issue that other cultural historians picked up and developed rewardingly. But the work's themes were all significant to the writing of histories of the period.

Other Ideas

While Eugene Genovese's ideas about the master–slave relationship dominate *Roll, Jordan, Roll: The World the Slaves Made*, there are several secondary ideas that add depth to his study of American antebellum* slavery:

1. The issue of race is important, although Genovese does not see it as the cause or the defining feature of slavery. He states early in the text that "the racial distinction between master and slave heightened the tension inherent in an unjust social order."[1]

> 66 The delicious irony of a committed Marxist saying anything so moving about religion notwithstanding, Genovese's lengthy discourse on religion was a watershed in American religious historiography. Few historians of any ideological bent had even studied southern religion at all, but things were changing. The 1970s was a dramatic decade in the field of southern religious history. 99
>
> Academic in Exile, "Weighing in on a Heavy-Weight: Genovese's *Roll, Jordan, Roll*"

For Genovese, racism was a secondary component in an unjust class system that placed slaveholders in positions of power over slaves.

2. In his exploration of slave culture, Genovese pays particular attention to slave religion. The role of religion, especially Christianity, illustrates Genovese's central thesis about the contradictory and paradoxical relationship between slaves and their masters. Religion serves as a means both to control the slaves and to allow slaves to carve out their own space of autonomy and resistance.

3. Genovese places antebellum slavery in a comparative context, showing that paternalism* was unique to American slavery. He argues that all instances of slavery come about to resolve a shortage of labor. But, he says, in the United States slavery developed particular features—the ideology of paternalism chief among them.

4. Genovese also discusses how American slavery restricted the development of capitalist social relations, in which wages and social classes, for example, are particularly significant. This enriches the contextual backdrop against which Genovese's

larger dramatic narrative plays out.

Exploring the Ideas

Race is a secondary idea for Genovese, and it is distinctly less important than class. He demonstrates this in two ways: in the context of the master–slave relationship itself, and in the relationship between slaveholders and white Southerners who did not own slaves.

Genovese notes that most of the cruelty to slaves was blamed on plantation overseers (supervisors) rather than on the slaveholders themselves. Overseers did not need to establish a paternalistic relationship, so they were much more likely to rule with brute force. By restricting the overseers' cruelty, slaveholders were able to maintain the safety of their working slave population and to pose as their slaves' paternalistic defenders. In a dispute, slaveholders would often believe the accounts from their black slaves, for example, rather than the white overseer. This reinforced their status position over both slave and overseer.[2] In describing the relationships that existed between Southern whites in the antebellum South, Genovese emphasizes the primacy of class.

In his discussion of slave culture and community, however, Genovese highlights the importance of religion.

Religion allowed slaves to develop a strong sense of personal worth through "the freedom and inviolability of the human soul." The slaves' own unique version of Christianity blended it with African spiritual beliefs. It created "an awareness of the moral limits of submission," and confirmed that "no man's will can become that of another unless he himself wills it—that the ideal of slavery cannot be realized, no matter how badly the body is broken and the spirit tormented."[3] Slave Christianity rejected the guilt-laden concept of original sin, merging the personas of Jesus and Moses to provide both deliverance and redemption. Slaves used religion to create a psychological defense against the cruelty of slavery.

Genovese also places antebellum Southern slavery into a

comparative context. This highlights the difference between American slavery and slavery in other nations, and indicates the difference between the free labor of the capitalist North and slave labor. This dual framework allows Genovese to emphasize the exceptional character of Southern paternalism.

Overlooked

Due to the impressive scope and close attention to detail of *Roll, Jordan, Roll*, there is little about the slave experience that Genovese does not touch upon. In the decades since the book was published, historians have followed up many themes that Genovese touched upon but did not fully explore. One area that needs more work is the degree of sexual violence perpetrated against slaves.

The American historian Diane Sommerville,* for example, discusses the under-researched area of the rape of female slaves. She notes that *Roll, Jordan, Roll* is one of the first books to address this subject.[4] In his brief discussions on miscegenation* (the mixing of different racial groups), Genovese provides evidence of sexual relationships between white masters and their slaves. But his interpretation of the evidence suggests a prevalence of consensual relationships. Sommerville rejects Genovese's romanticized approach, pointing to a growing body of work that focuses on the sexual abuse of female slaves.[5]

Yet the most overlooked aspect of *Roll, Jordan, Roll* is Genovese's central thesis: the dialectical* relationship between the slaveholders and the slaves (that is, the idea that each group was transformed through the process of resolving the oppositions between them in conflict). Historians are aware of the idea, but they have not pursued it. Instead, historians interested in the experience of slavery on the plantation have focused on looking at *either* slaves *or* slaveholders. Although most have followed Genovese's lead in examining slave culture and community, they commonly look at slaves in isolation, attempting to understand the experience of slavery from the slave's perspective.

NOTES

1   Eugene D. Genovese, *Roll, Jordan, Roll: The World the Slaves Made* (New York: Vintage Books, 1976), 4.

2   Genovese, *Roll, Jordan, Roll,* 17.

3   Genovese, *Roll, Jordan, Roll*, 283.

4   Dianne Miller Sommerville, "Moonlight, Magnolias, and Brigadoon; or, 'Almost Like Being in Love': Mastery and Sexual Exploitation in Eugene D. Genovese's Plantation South," *Radical History Review* 88, no. 4 (2004): 70.

5   George M. Fredrickson, "*Roll, Jordan, Roll: The World the Slaves Made,* by Eugene D. Genovese," *Journal of American History* 62, no. 1 (June 1975): 131; Genovese, *Roll, Jordan, Roll,* 413–31.

MODULE 7
ACHIEVEMENT

KEY POINTS

- Genovese's attempt to reexamine slavery from a Marxist*
  perspective, placing class at the heart of his analysis, proved
  highly successful.

- *Roll, Jordan, Roll*'s success as a work was founded on the
  complexity and subtlety of Genovese's theoretical approach
  and on the depth and quality of his empirical research—that
  is, research using evidence that can actually be observed and
  measured.

- The growth of analyses that emphasize race and gender in the
  writing of history has placed limits on the broader acceptance
  of Genovese's work.

Assessing the Argument

In *Roll, Jordan, Roll: The World the Slaves Made*, Eugene Genovese sets
out "to tell the story of slave life as accurately as possible." He aims to
examine the ways in which black people endured "one of history's
greatest crimes."[1] The book's subtitle—*The World the Slaves Made*—
makes it clear that Genovese intends *Roll, Jordan, Roll* to focus on the
slaves themselves, rather than simply on the slaveholders' perceptions
of them. And, indeed, he uses a number of sources to explore the
master–slave relationship from both sides.

As well as using the "white" sources that the American historian
Ulrich B. Phillips* relied on—plantation records, diaries, and travelers'
accounts, for example—Genovese also mines available slave narratives
(testimony from slaves and former slaves) and autobiographies. This
combination of sources allows him to investigate the experiences of

> 66 There is something which, from the current political perspective, is remarkably reactionary about Genovese's oeuvre, even in those books he published as a Marxist who once came out openly for the Viet Cong. But that was when it was still possible to be a left-wing radical without having to be politically correct. 99
>
> Paul Gottfried, "Eugene D. Genovese, R.I.P." *The American Conservative*

both classes. His in-depth research is a huge and widely recognized contribution to the scholarship on slavery. By adding the slave perspective, Genovese's work went beyond that of Phillips, but retained the important insight about paternalism* that Phillips had introduced.

Genovese places equal emphasis on both sides of the master–slave relationship. In doing so he manages to avoid the moralism of some revisionist* historians who, in their reinterpretation of accepted understandings of slavery, dismiss entirely the planter's perspective. Genovese does not wish to present a partial or favorable view of Southern planters but he does want to understand their motivations as a ruling class. He succeeds in doing this by demonstrating that the actions of the planters, like the actions of the slaves, can only be understood through looking at the dynamic relationship between these two groups. This insistence on interpreting the slave–master relationship as dialectical* is Genovese's greatest and most original contribution.

Achievement in Context

As an American Marxist* writing during the Cold War,* Genovese faced more difficulty having his work accepted than a liberal or conservative historian might have done, even if his theoretical method was not the hard, dogmatic approach adopted by other radicals. Genovese embraced a softer, culturally oriented Marxism and rejected the rigidities of economic determinism. For him, in other words, society was not entirely shaped by economics: culture played a part, too.

Indeed, he even disavowed Marxism, quoting Marx himself in asserting: "Je ne suis pas marxiste"—"I am not a Marxist."[2] By this he meant that, like Marx, he distanced himself from those Marxist historians who adopted the materialist conception of history (roughly, the idea that history is very fundamentally shaped by economics), thereby retreating into theory. For Genovese, theory was not enough: historians must, he believed, bury themselves in the empirical evidence found in the archives.

Among Genovese's writings, this empirical and objective approach is particularly true of *Roll, Jordan, Roll.* As one reviewer of the book notes, Genovese's indebtedness to Marxist theory "enriches the text without overpowering it" and "inspires but never orchestrates the central thesis."[3] His Marxism did not undermine his achievement, even in the hostile context in which *Roll, Jordan, Roll* was published— he was writing about the "world the slaves made" at a time when African Americans were actively protesting the discrimination they continued to face. Certainly, the civil rights movement* created a climate that was more open to the idea of understanding history from below.

The positive reception Genovese's book enjoyed was due, in large part, to the strength of his evidence and the depth, range, and scope of his research. The evidence Genovese marshaled to make his case was both groundbreaking and exemplary, especially in the close attention he paid to the perspective of the slaves themselves.

Limitations
Some historians criticize Genovese's failure to differentiate between types of American slavery. One reviewer suggests that Genovese generalizes too much: by treating all antebellum* slavery as essentially

the same, he has been accused of flattening out the conditions slaves faced. In reality, slaves labored on large or small plantations, in the upper or lower South, in the house or in the field. This flattening out necessarily stresses some aspects of Southern history at the expense of others.[4]

It should be noted that *Roll, Jordan, Roll* was published at a time when there was less sensitivity among historians to issues of race and gender, and this might serve to limit the book's appeal today.

Genovese was aware, nevertheless, of a growing concern about the portrayal of women, African Americans and other minorities in American history. Indeed, in its focus on black lives, culture, and agency, *Roll, Jordan, Roll* serves as an answer to some of these concerns. Yet Genovese grew increasingly uncomfortable about the restrictions placed on what could and could not be said. In the ongoing academic debate, his books came to seem increasingly outdated.

For example, Genovese uses the word "nigger" to refer to black people throughout the text, which has arguably limited the book's appeal in an academic environment that is much more sensitive today than it was back in 1974. But it should also be noted that he specifically acknowledges the problematic nature of the word's use:"I have used it myself when it seemed the best way to capture the spirit of a contemporary situation. The word is offensive, but I believe that its omission would only anesthetize subject matter infinitely more offensive."[5]

Some readers are put off by Genovese's descriptions of loyal black female house slaves, or "Mammies." These appear outdated at best.[6] Others are uncomfortable with his admiration for a Southern slaveholding class, a class which he himself holds accountable for "one of history's greatest crimes."[7]

NOTES

1   Eugene D. Genovese, *Roll, Jordan, Roll: The World the Slaves Made* (New York: Vintage Books, 1976), preface, xvi.

2   Eugene D. Genovese, "Marxian Interpretations of the Slave South," in *In Red and Black: Marxian Explorations in Southern and Afro-American History* (London: Vintage Books, 1971): 315.

3   Bertram Wyatt-Brown, "*Roll, Jordan Roll: The World the Slaves Made*, by Eugene D. Genovese," *Journal of Southern History* 41, no. 2 (1975): 240–2.

4   George M. Fredrickson, "*Roll, Jordan, Roll: The World the Slaves Made,* by Eugene D. Genovese," *Journal of American History* 62, no. 1 (June 1975): 131–3.

5   Genovese, *Roll, Jordan, Roll*, xvii.

6   Genovese, *Roll, Jordan, Roll*, 343–65.

7   Genovese, *Roll, Jordan, Roll*, xvi.

MODULE 8
PLACE IN THE AUTHOR'S WORK

KEY POINTS

- Genovese was one of the finest and most respected historians of the institution of slavery and of the American South.

- *Roll, Jordan, Roll* was Genovese's fourth and most celebrated work. The book showed a maturity that built on his earlier investigations of slavery; it leant more on deep archival research than on the more rigid Marxist* categories of his earlier work, and it fed into a cultural zeitgeist* (that is, "spirit of the time") that privileged the perspective of oppressed groups.

- The book placed Genovese's name among the top rank of American historians of his generation. His earlier work built up to it. His later work never managed to surpass it in quality, insight, or breadth.

Positioning

Roll, Jordan, Roll: The World the Slaves Made was Eugene Genovese's fourth book and his second monograph about slavery. It was also the culmination of many years of research. Nine years earlier, in 1965, Genovese had published a collection of essays called *The Political Economy of Slavery*. These essays presented a distinctly Marxist interpretation of the institution of slavery. Avoiding moral judgment, they examined the profitability or otherwise of slave labor. Genovese's conclusion was that slavery was a remarkably inefficient, unprofitable, and backward system.

> 66 Genovese's Marxism, informed by his astute reading of Gramsci (long before this was fashionable), helped him delineate how the [slave-owning classes] developed a hegemonic worldview in defense of a social order based on human bondage. Most provocatively, Genovese insisted that his readers take the southern defense of slavery seriously as an authentic expression of class rule, rather than as a hypocritical pretense designed to paper over naked human exploitation and greed. 99
>
> Alex Lichtenstein, "Right Church, Wrong Pew: Eugene Genovese and Southern Conservatism." *New Politics*

In 1969 he brought out his first monograph on slavery, *The World the Slaveholders Made*. This homed in on what would become Genovese's lifelong obsession—the world view of the Southern planter class (that is, the slave-owning class). Although Genovese's many later works explored aspects of slavery and Southern life, he returned time and again to the outlook of the dominant planter class.

In 1971 Genovese published a second collection of essays, *In Red and Black*. These essays show how Genovese thought the historiography* of slavery was developing. They laid the analytical foundations for his seminal, or groundbreaking, work of 1974, *Roll, Jordan, Roll*.

Genovese was as controversial outside academia as he was within it. He first came to public notice in 1965 when he proclaimed his support for the Vietcong* in the Vietnam War* during a lecture at an antiwar protest on the Rutgers campus. His comments led to accusations of treason and calls to have him removed from his post. Genovese survived the controversy and remained an outspoken contrarian for his entire life. As American campus culture moved to the political left, he gradually moved to the right, and in 1995 he rejected leftist politics altogether, converting to conservative Catholicism. Even in the 1960s he had been impatient with many aspects of left-wing activism in the United States, such as the charged discussions relating to sexual or racial identity and what he perceived to be claims to victimhood. By the 1990s, his impatience had turned to intolerance. Yet despite his political shift from radicalism to conservatism, his intellectual approach remained coherent.

Integration

The most important thread running through Genovese's work is the primacy of class in the history of the antebellum* South. Although he was interested in both sides of the master–slave class relationship, he argued that the world view of the planter class was the dominating influence.

Genovese's central concern was to understand why and how slavery lasted so long, within a political economy that was failing. How did a class based on the exploitation of slave labor exist so long inside a nation dedicated to freedom? His answer was that, in the nineteenth century, planter paternalism* offered an alternative world view to, and an implicit critique of, the liberal and republican free-labor ethos of the capitalist* North. Genovese locates in the Southern planter psyche a rich conservative tradition of political thought. This world view opposed the liberal capitalism that characterized the rest of the United States.

In the later years of his life, Genovese turned away from Marxism toward conservative Catholicism. He rejected mainstream academic life as too theory driven and politically correct.[1] The enthusiasm Genovese demonstrated for Southern proslavery intellectuals and his fascination with the role of religion defined the rest of his career. He continued to explore the cultural power of planter paternalism[2] in works such as the *Fruits of Merchant Capital* (1983), *The Mind of the Master Class* (2005), and *Fatal Deception: Slaveholding Paternalism in the*

Old South (2011). These were all co-written with his wife, the feminist American historian Elizabeth Fox-Genovese.* He also looked at the other side of the class equation in *From Rebellion to Revolution* (1979), in which he explains the low incidence of slave revolt in comparison with slave societies existing elsewhere in the Western hemisphere.

Significance

Despite his many later publications and the controversy surrounding his own political outlook, Genovese remains best known for *Roll, Jordan, Roll*. The book combines penetrating insights into the nature of planter paternalism with an extensive investigation of the ways in which slaves experienced and responded to slavery. It also includes a massive amount of empirical data supporting Genovese's findings. Indeed, the American historian Steven Hahn argues:

"[No] book of Genovese's has had the impact of *Roll, Jordan, Roll* … A long, complex, almost Hegelian* treatment of the master–slave relation—and of the dynamics of power that were embedded within it … Replete with comparative and international references, political allusions, and literary flourishes, *Roll, Jordan, Roll* may well be the finest work on slavery ever produced."[3]

An outspoken Marxist critic and a respected scholar of slavery before the publication of *Roll, Jordan, Roll*, the book elevated Genovese to the top rank of American historians—but his reputation has diminished considerably since then. After he repudiated Marxism and embraced Catholicism and conservatism, liberal academics found it easier to dismiss him and his work. The historian Peter Kolchin* noted in 2003 that admiration for Genovese's work was no longer fashionable. In contrast with his controversial past, according to Kolchin, "Eugene Genovese's name is no longer likely to elicit instant public recognition, and when it does, it is more often as a symbol of a quirky brand of conservatism than as a cutting-edge scholar of slavery."[4]

This has as much to do with Genovese's own rejection of what he saw as the increasingly intolerant culture of academic life as it does with academic rejection of his work. Today, his work, including *Roll, Jordan, Roll*, is still viewed by many historians of slavery as essential reading—albeit through a highly critical lens.

NOTES

1   Gary Nash, "Think Tank; A Rebellion Against History's Fuzzy Future," *New York Times,* May 2, 1998, accessed June 30, 2015, http://www.nytimes.com/1998/05/02/arts/think-tank-a-rebellion-against-history-s-fuzzy-future.html.

2   Peter Kolchin, "*Fatal Self-Deception: Slaveholding Paternalism in the Old South,* by Eugene D. Genovese and Elizabeth Fox-Genovese," *Civil War History* 59, no. 2 (June 2013): 242–3, accessed August 11, 2015, http://muse.jhu.edu/login?auth=0&type=summary&url=/journals/civil_war_history/v059/59.2.kolchin.html.

3   Steven Hahn, "From Radical to Right-Wing: The Legacy of Eugene Genovese," *The New Republic*, October 2, 2012, accessed June 30, 2015, http://www.newrepublic.com/article/books-and-arts/108044/radical-right-wing-the-legacy-eugene-genovese.

4   Peter Kolchin, "Eugene D. Genovese: Historian of Slavery," *Radical History Review* 88 (Winter 2004): 52–4.

SECTION 3
IMPACT

THE FIRST RESPONSES

KEY POINTS

- The immediate critical reception of *Roll, Jordan, Roll* was overwhelmingly positive. However, some scholars expressed reservations about Eugene Genovese's Marxist* perspective, his generosity toward the slaveholder's position, and his emphasis on white power over black agency.

- Genovese responded to criticisms by critiquing his critics: he explained why understanding the planter class was so crucial to understanding the nature of slavery.

- The most important factor shaping the book's reception was the growth of a desire for a "bottom-up" perspective that was a result of the activist leanings of some social historians: for some, *Roll, Jordan, Roll* satisfied this; for others, it did not go far enough.

Criticism

Historians responded positively to the publication of Eugene Genovese's *Roll, Jordan, Roll: The World the Slaves Made*. They applauded the depth and breadth of the sources he engaged, his innovative dialectical* approach, and the vast chronological and geographical sweep of the book.[1] Many scholars praised the book for its comprehensiveness, and many agreed with the American historian Charles Dew* when he said that *Roll, Jordan, Roll* would "almost certainly take its place as one of the commanding works in [historical studies] of American Negro slavery."[2]

The three central criticisms of the book relate to Genovese's analytical framework, his treatment of the actions and ideas of the

❝ Gutman's view [is] that he, Gutman, was writing the history of the real lives and feelings of working people, especially black people, in direct opposition to Genovese's preoccupation with abstract ideas and power. Presumably those who have read Roll, Jordan, Roll can recognize that distortion for themselves. Certainly, most people—serious historians and informed general readers alike—know that power has precisely to do with the lives and feelings of working people. ❞

John Womack, Lou Ferlerger, and Robert Paquette, "Roll, Jordan, Roll." *New York Review of Books*

planter class, and his treatment of the actions and ideas of the slaves. The American historian Richard King* indicated the "lack of fit" between Genovese's Marxist categories and the slave South.[3] George Fredrickson,* an American historian known for his careful, comparative approach, worried that Genovese's model of master–slave relations did not differentiate between different forms of slavery:"Like all models or analogies, Genovese's obscures the uniqueness of the phenomenon under study in order to subsume it under a more general category."[4]

Most criticism, however, was directed at Genovese's portrayal of one side or other of the master–slave relationship. Reviewers thought Genovese was too generous to the planter class.They argued that he did slaves a disservice by suggesting that they accepted the planters' cultural world view. The objections of the American historians Herbert Gutman* and John Blassingame* stand out. Both were important pioneers of the New Social History,* an approach to the writing of history that began from the viewpoint of the oppressed.

Gutman chided Genovese for writing about the slave quarters

from the verandah of the big house, arguing against the idea that slave culture was only "reactive" to planter paternalism.* Gutman proposed a more active and creative role for slaves in carrying their culture from Africa.[5] Similarly, Blassingame was concerned that by "always beginning his discussions with the way the master defined a situation, Genovese limited his ability to see how the slave defined it."[6]

Responses

Roll, Jordan, Roll received critical acclaim and in 1975 won the Bancroft Prize, a prestigious literary award for books about US history. This encouraged Genovese, who dismissed objections to his Marxist analysis, calling them "bourgeois" (that is, middle class and content with the capitalist* system). He also denied that he had imposed a theoretical uniformity on the "peculiar institution" of slavery: "I do not believe, and have never asserted, that the Old South should be understood as a monolith. The very idea must be repellent to anyone conversant with Marxism."[7] He denied overstating the positive role of paternalism, stating: "I am at a loss to understand how anyone could read me as saying that paternalism generated black culture." Rather, Genovese clarified: "Paternalism played a constructive role only to the extent that the slaves waged a determined struggle to transform it according to their own light." He was horrified at the charge that he was too "soft" on the planters or that he underestimated the horrors of slavery. On the contrary, he argued, he hoped to highlight the slaves' ability to retain their humanity—their courage, self-discipline, and selflessness—and that "the extraordinary achievement of black people in their struggle for spiritual as well as physical survival constitutes an important reference point for our time."[8]

Genovese also denied ever characterizing the antebellum* South as "seignorial"—that is, he denied claiming that it recalled the medieval social system of feudalism—as some critics claim he did. Genovese suggested that the slave South was neither feudal nor capitalist and that, instead, the rise of a slaveholding class with regional political power created a unique society.

Conflict and Consensus

Two distinct schools formed in the debate about the Southern political economy and the nature of planter rule. Genovese headed one group, which argued that the South was precapitalist* with a paternalistic elite. The American historian Herbert G. Gutman* led the challengers to this group, arguing instead that the South was capitalist, and that slave labor experienced forms of exploitation similar to those of the industrial working class in the Northern states.

The clash between Genovese and Gutman became political and personal as well as a matter for academics working in the field of history, and the attacks grew quite acrimonious. Historian Ira Berlin* noted that both Gutman and Genovese rejected "wooden determinism"* and that both "came to see culture as the terrain of class warfare." However, "while Gutman viewed the struggle from the bottom, Genovese saw it from the top."[9] It was, in essence, a struggle between types of history. Gutman was a spokesman for the New Social History, which emphasizes the lived experience of ordinary people— and which was an approach to history that Genovese abhorred.

Although *Roll, Jordan, Roll* is still widely regarded as one of the very best books on slavery, historians of slavery from the next generation almost universally adopted Gutman's approach of writing history "from the bottom up," focusing their attention on the slave experience and the creation of slave culture. Historians like John Blassingame* and Lawrence Levine* promoted the study of slave lives from the perspectives of the slaves themselves. In the next generation, feminist historians directed a new criticism at *Roll, Jordan, Roll.* As the field of women's history took off, Genovese's work began to be assessed for its portrayal of women and the way it approached gender issues.

NOTES

1   See, for example, Bertram Wyatt-Brown, "*Roll, Jordan Roll: The World the Slaves Made,* by Eugene D. Genovese," *Journal of Southern History* 41, no. 2 (May 1975): 240–2; and George M. Fredrickson, "*Roll, Jordan, Roll: The World the Slaves Made,* by Eugene D. Genovese," *Journal of American History* 62, no. 1 (June 1975): 132.

2   Charles B. Dew, "The Sambo and Nat Turner in Everyslave: A Review of *Roll, Jordan, Roll,*" *Civil War History* 21, no. 3 (September 1975): 261–8.

3   Richard H. King, "Marxism and the Slave South," *American Quarterly* 29, no. 1 (Spring 1977): 117–31.

4   Fredrickson, "*Roll, Jordan, Roll,*" 132.

5   Herbert G. Gutman, *The Black Family in Slavery and Freedom* (New York: Vintage Books, 1977), 303–26.

6   John W. Blassingame, "*Roll, Jordan, Roll: The World the Slaves Made,* by Eugene D. Genovese," *Journal of Social History* 9, no. 3 (Spring 1976): 403–9.

7   Eugene D. Genovese, "A Reply to Criticism," *Radical History Review* 13 (1977): 94–114.

8   Genovese, "A Reply to Criticism," 108.

9   Ira Berlin, "Introduction: Herbert G. Gutman and the American Working Class," in Herbert G. Gutman, *Power and Culture: Essays on the American Working Class* (New York: Pantheon Books, 1987): 48.

MODULE 10
THE EVOLVING DEBATE

KEY POINTS

- Genovese's concept of planter paternalism* provoked much scholarship—but largely that scholarship was seeking to disprove his thesis.

- The vast majority of historians worked to disprove Genovese's claims about the role of the planter class by uncovering an autonomous slave culture.

- Genovese's approach has become outmoded; historians who followed him have placed an ever-larger focus on the agency of oppressed groups, rather than looking at the power structures they lived within.

Uses and Problems

In *Roll, Jordan, Roll: The World the Slaves Made* Eugene Genovese argues that slaveholders felt a profound sense of guilt about owning slaves that forced them to perform all kinds of psychological acrobatics to justify slavery. Historians such as Herbert Gutman* and James Anderson* thought this interpretation suggested sympathy for, or even an admiration of, the slaveholders. This perceived bias prevented many scholars developing Genovese's ideas. Spurred on by what he saw as widespread—possibly willful—misinterpretation of his ideas, Genovese developed and deepened his arguments about the planter class. He published several critically acclaimed works about the Southern slaveholding class and paternalism well into his old age. His final work on the subject, *Fatal Self-Deception: Slaveholding Paternalism in the Old South*, was published in 2011, just a year before his death.

Despite these rebuttals, however, the criticism that he was too soft

> ❝ As Marxist scholarship flourished, the modifications and multiplications multiplied to the point that the coherence and distinctiveness of what remained became very doubtful. With the increasing emphasis on culture and consciousness, how far back did one have to reach to find materialist determination 'in the last instance'? ❞
>
> Peter Novick, *That Noble Dream*

on the planters persisted.

Younger historians objected that Genovese's master–slave dialectic* denied slaves their full measure of agency and autonomy. John Blassingame* denied Genovese's idea that slaves internalized white values such as paternalism: "Rather than identifying with and submitting totally to his master, the slave held onto many remnants of his African culture, gained a sense of worth in the quarters, spent most of his time free from surveillance by whites, controlled important aspects of his life, and did some personally meaningful things on his own volition."[1] In a 2002 review essay, the American historian James Anderson sums up the critique: "*Roll, Jordan, Roll* is presented as a book about slaves and the world they made. In actuality it is an attempt to capture the slave experience through an analysis of white paternalistic hegemony."[2] Today, Genovese is out of fashion. Contemporary readings of his work begin with a rejection of his central ideas.[3]

Schools of Thought

Genovese contends that the world view of the slaveholding class lay at the heart of American slavery. But scholars of slavery suggest that the South was not as monolithic as Genovese's analysis implied. They also flip Genovese's master–slave analogy; that is, they investigate those people at the bottom—the slaves—rather than those at the top—the planters.

The historian James Oakes* presents a particularly prominent response to Genovese. In *The Ruling Race: A History of American Slaveholders* (1982)[4] Oakes accepts Genovese's concept of paternalism for the leading planters on large plantations but questions, however, whether these elite planters were representative of the class. Oakes's own study concentrated on the majority of slaveholding farmers who owned "perhaps a handful" of slaves. It was these middle-class planters, he suggests, who shaped the character of the South.[5] Although Oakes makes a strong case, the historian James Roark* judges *The Ruling Race* an inadequate challenge to *Roll, Jordan, Roll*: "Any attempt to refute Eugene Genovese's complex interpretation of the antebellum South must confront directly the crucial issues of class and power, and this Oakes does not do."[6]

Other scholars have set out to demonstrate the autonomous—that is, independent and self-governing—nature of slave culture in smaller, local studies of slavery, concentrating on particular slave communities, regions, or themes. For example, Charles Joyner's* book *Down by the Riverside: A South Carolina Slave Community* (1985) draws on anthropology, folklore, and oral history to reconstruct the culture of a slave community. Joyner's book, like Genovese's, takes its title from a slave spiritual, but Joyner emphasizes the creolization (that is, roughly, the fusion into something distinctive and new) of African traditions over and above the influence of the planter class on slave culture. Many scholars address themes that Genovese first drew attention to—such as planter ideology or slave religion—and take them in new directions.

In Current Scholarship

Although historians of slavery have not embraced Genovese's class-based Marxist* approach to slavery, they have followed him in other ways. Historians in many fields use the concept of cultural hegemony* to explain elite influence and power. For instance, the Indian-born American historian Manisha Sinha* suggests that it is a concept better applied to white Southern society than to slaves, since "the pervasiveness of proslavery sentiments among church leaders, newspaper editors, and politicians gives ample proof of slaveholders' ideological and political domination in the Old South."[7] Sinha's cultural interpretation is stripped of class politics and Marxist ideology. As a result, Genovese's influence on her work is barely recognizable—but it is still present, albeit in this disguised or altered form.

Where Genovese sparked debate and disagreement, he also sparked further research. For instance, Oakes's work on the planter class takes Genovese's claims as his starting point, drawing different conclusions. For instance, whereas Genovese suggests that the antebellum* South became more paternalistic during the course of the nineteenth century, in contrast, Oakes concludes that the region moved gradually away from paternalism over the century.

The historian Michael Gomez* dismisses Genovese's analysis of slave religion as "functionalist" (that is, as founded on the idea that all aspects of a culture must necessarily serve some kind of function) and rejects paternalism as a useful framework for understanding black culture.[8] But historians of slavery continue to engage with the concept of paternalism even if they disagree with Genovese's application of it.

NOTES

1   John Blassingame, *The Slave Community: Plantation Life in the Antebellum South* (New York: Oxford University Press, 1979): xii.

2   James D. Anderson, "Aunt Jemima in Dialectics: Genovese on Slave Culture," *Journal of African American History* 87 (Winter 2002): 105.

3   Peter Kolchin, "Eugene D. Genovese: Historian of Slavery," *Radical History Review* 88 (Winter 2004), 59.

4   James Oakes, *The Ruling Race: A History of American Slaveholders* (London: New York: W. W. Norton, 1998).

5   Oakes, *The Ruling Race,* 51.

6   James L. Roark, "*The Ruling Race: A History of American Slaveholders* by James Oakes,"*American Historical Review* 88, no. 4 (October 1983): 1067.

7   Manisha Sinha, "Eugene D. Genovese: The Mind of a Marxist Conservative," *Radical History Review* 88 (Winter 2004): 10–11.

8   Michael A. Gomez, *Exchanging Our Country Marks: The Transformation of African Identities in the Colonial and Antebellum South* (Chapel Hill: University of North Carolina Press, 1998).

IMPACT AND INFLUENCE TODAY

KEY POINTS

- Historians still hold *Roll, Jordan, Roll* in very high regard. Despite its limitations, many see it as the best book ever published on American slavery.

- Genovese challenges historians to understand the character of Southern antebellum society, to explain how and why slavery survived so long, and to assess the relationship between slaves and their masters.

- One position adopted by Genovese's challengers is that slave society was capitalistic* rather than paternalistic;* another is that slaves developed their own culture in an entirely autonomous (that is, independent) way.

Position

Eugene Genovese's *Roll, Jordan, Roll: The World the Slaves Made* has left a lasting legacy. The American historian Peter Kolchin* outlines four overlapping areas of research directly influenced by Genovese, noting that "no one has had a bigger role in shaping [the] basic contours" of the vast and varied literature on American slavery.[1] For Kolchin, Genovese's work inspired or enlivened four debates in the field of written history:

- The debate about the political economy of the antebellum South. Was it profitable? Capitalist? Feudal?
- The debate about the character of slaveholders' thought. Was it racist or paternalistic?
- The debate about the culture and experience of slave communities, especially their religious beliefs.

> ❝ Few historians have left their mark on a field as decisively as Eugene D. Genovese. The shape of southern history, particularly slavery studies, would look rather different without his substantial corpus. Debates in southern history continue to be framed around the issues first raised or developed by Genovese in his early work on the Old South and slavery. More than any other historian of slavery, he has set the agenda for antebellum* southern historiography and bears responsibility for both its strengths and its limitations. ❞
>
> Manisha Sinha, "Eugene D. Genovese: The Mind of a Marxist Conservative"

- The debate about American slavery in comparison with other instances of slavery.

Although Kolchin is a prominent scholar of slavery and admits to being a longtime admirer of Genovese's work, he recognizes that this is "not now a fashionable assertion."[2] But he notes that the aim of the "Genovese Forum," the selection of criticism and commentary on Genovese's work in the journal *Radical History Review*, to which his essay is a contribution, was to reinvigorate discussion about the historian's work and, by doing so, make clear the debt owed to Genovese by those working in the field of slavery studies.

Whether or not one agrees with him, Genovese's meticulous research means that *Roll, Jordan, Roll* is still of value. Although newer research dealing with topics such as slave gender and sexuality, for example, is less indebted to Genovese, *Roll, Jordan, Roll* is still cited by gender historians as igniting their interest in the field. Indeed, the American historian Diane Sommerville* cites the book as "the most important book published in Southern history" despite being "one of the most misogynistic and least sympathetic discussions of female slaves to be found in the modern literature on American slavery." Like other critics, Sommerville says Genovese romanticizes the master and excuses such sins as rape.[3]

Interaction

Historians working in the New Social History* (an approach to historical analysis that begins with low-status, generally oppressed, people) offered most of the challenges to Genovese's work in the years following the publication of *Roll, Jordan, Roll*. They objected to the way he seems to place slave culture in direct and subordinate relation to planter ideology. But they also recognized his contribution in opening up this field of study to closer analysis.

Genovese challenged the historian Stanley Elkins's* depiction of the slave victim as a childlike, tactically compliant "sambo" by emphasizing the existence of both accommodation and resistance within slave communities. His own critics went further. They have concentrated on the resistance slaves marshaled. Herbert Gutman,* Genovese's fiercest critic, argues that slaves made a life for themselves "using cultural forms that whites did not even perceive—much less impose, promote or concede to them as part of a paternalistic compromise."[4]

Social and cultural historians studying slavery pursued this line of enquiry for a generation after Genovese. They focus on the autonomous slave culture, emphasizing slave agency and paying little heed to the masters or the power structures that surrounded slaves. For example, one area of this research focuses on slave religion and argues that African beliefs had a greater influence on slave spirituality than planter Christianity.

When New Social History gave way to poststructuralism,* the historical focus changed again. Historians who adopt the poststructuralist approach, which rejects the validity of either/or oppositions in the analysis of cultural systems, are often interested in looking at recurring themes within cultures and how those cultures express their ideas and beliefs. Marxism* and other forms of social science have become unfashionable among cultural historians within slavery studies. Questions of gender, sexuality, and identity have replaced interest in class, power, and politics.

The Continuing Debate

In the 1990s, Genovese moved away from Marxism. He converted to conservative Catholicism[5] and became an outspoken critic of political correctness* among academics. He co-founded—and presided over—the Historical Society, intended to be an alternative to the mainstream professional associations—the American Historical Association and the Organization of American Historians.[6] But as Genovese turned away from mainstream historical academia, he fell out of favor with his colleagues in the field.

Since the 1970s historical debate and research have led to far greater knowledge about the nature of the antebellum South. While Genovese's approach centered on intellectual and political history, subsequent scholars have employed methods and approaches from social history and cultural history. Others have examined American slavery in the context of the global development of capitalism. Historian Edward Baptist's* *The Half has Never Been Told* (2014) argues that, far from being precapitalist,* as Genovese claimed, antebellum slavery was the foundation on which American capitalism was built. The cotton trade was an important pillar of American economic power.[7]

The debate about slavery was passionate in the immediate wake of the civil rights movement,* with some historians taking a very critical line against Genovese. But from the start of the twenty-first century, scholars have taken a more sober approach. Historians started reassessing Genovese in light of his positive contributions. Some scholars of slave religion and gender relations find much that is wanting in his work, but there is also increased recognition of its value.

Historians have called for renewed discussion of Genovese's corpus, to explore new ways in which his findings could be used.[8] In 2011 Princeton University hosted a conference called "Slavery and Southern History: The Work of Eugene Genovese." This brought the most important of Genovese's ideas back to the fore of historiographical* debate—namely, the concept of the master–slave relationship.[9]

NOTES

1   Peter Kolchin, "Eugene D. Genovese: Historian of Slavery," *Radical History Review* 88 (Winter 2004): 54.

2   Kolchin, "Eugene D. Genovese," 52.

3   Dianne Miller Sommerville, "Moonlight, Magnolias, and Brigadoon; or, 'Almost Like Being in Love': Mastery and Sexual Exploitation in Eugene D. Genovese's Plantation South," *Radical History Review* 88, no. 4 (2004): 68–82.

4   George M. Frederickson, *The Arrogance of Race* (Middletown, CT: Wesleyan University Press, 1989): 117.

5   Douglas Martin, "Eugene D. Genovese, Historian of South, Dies at 82," *New York Times*, September 29, 2012, accessed June 30, 2015, http://www.nytimes.com/2012/09/30/us/eugene-d-genovese-historian-of-south-dies-at-82.html?_r=0.

6   Martin, "Eugene D. Genovese"; Gary Nash, "Think Tank; A Rebellion Against History's Fuzzy Future," *New York Times*, May 2, 1998, accessed June 30, 2015, http://www.nytimes.com/1998/05/02/arts/think-tank-a-rebellion-against-history-s-fuzzy-future.html.

7   Edward E. Baptist, *Half Has Never Been Told: Slavery and the Making of American Capitalism* (New York: Basic Books, 2014).

8   Peter Kolchin et al., "Genovese Forum," *Radical History Review* 88 (Winter 2004).

9   Alexander Hamilton Institute for the Study of Western Civilization and the Center for African American Studies, "Slavery and Southern History: The Work of Eugene Genovese," Conference, Princeton University, March 25, 2011, http://web.princeton.edu/sites/jmadison/calendar/documents/2011%200325%20Genovese%20Brochure%20%282%29.pdf. Conference video: http://vimeo.com/album/1629546.

WHERE NEXT?

KEY POINTS

- *Roll, Jordan, Roll* is likely to remain an influential text in the study of American slavery.

- Scholars will continue to benefit from Genovese's insights into the master–slave relationship, slave culture, and religion in the antebellum* South.

- The text is seminal because it combines a mastery of the sources with a sophisticated and innovative methodology, and deep insights into the nature and meaning of slavery in America.

Potential

Eugene Genovese's *Roll, Jordan, Roll: The World the Slaves Made* is a significant work in the history of slavery. The depth and scope of his research and his sophisticated analysis of an extensive range of sources mean *Roll, Jordan, Roll* has yet to be surpassed as an investigation of slavery in the American South. While critics have taken issue with Genovese's central theoretical framework—the dialectical* relationship between master and slave—the importance of the book means that, decades after its publication, it continues to be read and referenced by scholars in the field.[1]

Genovese died in 2012. In the years before his death, both established and emerging scholars participated in two important symposia acknowledging his contribution to the field. In 2004, the respected publication *Radical History Review* published a forum of historiographical* debate on Genovese's work. In 2011, Princeton University hosted a retrospective reassessment of Genovese's thought.

> ❝ [Those] of us who disagree with Genovese's newfound ideology would do well to take his ideas seriously, just as he took seriously the views of those with whom he disagreed, because the issues that trouble him are serious ones for which no one has yet put forth satisfactory answers. [It] is important not to read backward from his current political pronouncements so as to tar his existing scholarship on slavery, which must be judged on its own merits. As I have argued, this scholarship is central to the massive reinterpretation of slavery that we have seen over the past three decades, a reinterpretation still very much ongoing. ❞
>
> Peter Kolchin, "Eugene D. Genovese: Historian of Slavery"

When Genovese died, despite the relationship he had with other historians that was at times frosty, many obituaries expressed admiration for his scholarly achievements. This all suggests that his work—and particularly the meticulously researched *Roll, Jordan, Roll*—will have a long legacy. Most scholars reject Genovese's political commitments—both his early-career Marxism* and his later conservatism—but continue to learn from his scholarly contribution.

Future Directions

The field of slavery studies remains dynamic. Historians have moved away from Genovese's focus on master–slave relations to ask new questions about new areas, such as gender. The American historian Diane Sommerville* recently criticized *Roll, Jordan, Roll* for being "bourgeois" in its interpretation of gender relations (ironically, given Genovese's Marxist approach, "bourgeois" is a term used in Marxist analysis to refer to the middle class, but one that is steeped in the social values of capitalism*). Somerville argues that Genovese "utterly fails to comprehend how slave owners exercised power over their female slaves ... he continually interprets power as love, romanticizing power—and what could be more bourgeois than that?"[2]

The British historian Emily West* also seeks to correct some of Genovese's outdated gender stereotypes in her work. But even she thinks that *Roll, Jordan, Roll* "will remain a key text." She believes it represents "a pivotal moment in slavery historiography when historians turned from thinking about enslavers to the enslaved."[3]

Other historians have changed the scope of the study of slavery. Michael Gomez* dismisses Genovese's analysis of slave religion as "functionalist" (that is, as assuming that everything exists in a society to serve some function), noting that "the African was more or less helpless, in Genovese's imagination, and could not resist the incursion of Christian thought and beliefs."[4] Gomez argues for more focus on the agency of slaves. Meanwhile, the historian Edward Baptist* suggests that studying the *international* slave trade brings new insights for scholars.

However, Genovese does have advocates. One is the historian Peter Kolchin.* While not denying that Genovese's work has become unfashionable, Kolchin concludes that Genovese "still sets the terms of the debate, even for those who are least persuaded ... but I would go further: I believe that in many respects, his writings on slavery continue to persuade as well."[5]

As scholars and teachers of the current generation are keeping Genovese's influence alive, it is possible that future historians will rediscover the importance of his insights. Genovese is being cited in fields of slavery studies outside the antebellum South. Caribbean specialists, for example, have referenced his work on religion, resistance, and paternalism.*[6] In a field with a global outlook, Genovese may remain influential.

Summary

Roll, Jordan, Roll is Eugene Genovese's best and most sophisticated work. Combining a rich use of historical sources with penetrating interpretation, the book uses extensive research to explain how the political economy of the slave South survived for so long.

Genovese's focus on both sides of the master–slave relationship explores how that relationship both reinforced and challenged the power structures of slavery. Genovese claims that the master's paternalism both provided slaveholders with a comforting justification of slavery and forced them to see the humanity of their slaves. Genovese also described how slaves responded to white cultural impositions, such as Christianity, by reinterpreting their meanings and using them to confirm their own humanity.

The book deserves to be read for its multi-layered complexity, which might encourage students to think in ways they may not have thought before. It is worth noting that in his sweeping survey of American slavery, the American historian Ira Berlin* cites *Roll, Jordan, Roll* as the place that scholars interested in the "vast scholarship" of both paternalism and slave revolts should start. Berlin points to five classic texts in the field, *Roll, Jordan, Roll* among them. He claims that the book "elevated the history of slavery—and all of American history—by his seeing the slaves as a class in, and occasionally for, themselves."[7] The book, like all good histories, was about the future as much as it was about the past.

NOTES

1   Manisha Sinha, "Eugene D. Genovese: The Mind of a Marxist Conservative," *Radical History Review* 88 (Winter 2004): 10, 16.

2   Dianne Miller Sommerville, "Moonlight, Magnolias, and Brigadoon; or, 'Almost Like Being in Love': Mastery and Sexual Exploitation in Eugene D. Genovese's Plantation South," *Radical History Review* 88, no. 4 (2004): 80.

3   Emily West, *Enslaved Women in America: From Colonial Times to Emancipation* (Lanham, MD: Rowman & Littlefield, 2014); email correspondence with Emily West, "Genovese," June 23, 2015.

4   Michael A. Gomez, *Exchanging Our Country Marks: The Transformation of African Identities in the Colonial and Antebellum South* (Chapel Hill: University of North Carolina Press, 1998), 246.

5   Peter Kolchin, "Eugene D. Genovese: Historian of Slavery," *Radical History Review* 88 (Winter 2004), 64.

6   David Barry Gaspar, *Bondmen and Rebels: A Study of Master–Slave Relations in Antigua* (Durham, NC: Duke University Press, 1993); Michael Craton, *Testing the Chains: Resistance to Slavery in the British West Indies* (Ithaca, NY: Cornell University Press, 2009): 249.

7   Ira Berlin, *Many Thousands Gone: The First Two Centuries of Slavery in North America* (Cambridge, MA: Harvard University Press, 1998), 487.

GLOSSARY

GLOSSARY OF TERMS

American Civil War: a civil conflict fought between the Republican North and the Confederate South of the USA between 1861 and 1865, after the Southern states left the Union on the election of Abraham Lincoln as US president. The South surrendered in 1865 to a victorious North; slavery was almost immediately abolished by constitutional amendment.

American Left: a fragmentary and diverse political grouping, broadly committed to social equality and civil rights for poor and disadvantaged groups. The "old" left is associated with economic, labor, and welfare issues, while the "new" left focused more on cultural, gender, and racial issues.

Antebellum: from the Latin, meaning "pre-war," and usually referring to the Old South or the American South before the American Civil War (1861–65).

Capitalism: an economic system based on private ownership, private enterprise, and the maximization of profit.

Civil rights: those legal rights pertaining to the free exercise of citizenship in a democracy, such as freedom of movement, freedom to own property, and freedom to vote.

Civil rights movement: a broad-based movement in America aimed at abolishing racial discrimination and supporting equal legal and political rights for African Americans. The focus was on eradicating racial segregation in law and on giving African Americans, especially in the South, access to the vote.

Cold War: a period of tension from 1945 to 1990 that existed between the capitalist United States and the communist Soviet Union, together with nations aligned to each.

Communist: an ideological and political supporter of the creation of a communist society in which workers jointly own the means of production; a member of the Communist Party.

Communist Party USA: a communist political party established in the United States in 1919. Its membership has always been small, although it enjoyed some notoriety and popularity in the 1930s; it has never had an elected party representative in either state or federal government.

Cultural hegemony: a Marxist term describing the process whereby the ruling class manipulates the cultural outlook of a diverse society (that is, their beliefs, values, and understandings) so that this ruling class's world view becomes the generally accepted norm; in effect, it makes what is actually coercive rule appear to be consensual rule.

Determinism: the doctrine that everything, including human action, is ultimately determined by factors that are seen as being external to the will.

Dialectical: a Marxian process of change through conflict, whereby two opposing forces or classes are transformed through the process of interactive conflict into an aspect of a new contradiction.

Hegelianism: the term given to the philosophy of German philosopher G.W. F. Hegel. Hegel developed the notion of the master–slave dialectic. Karl Marx embraced Hegel's theory of history but replaced his idealistic dialectics with material dialectics.

Historiography: a body of historical work, usually constituting a debate within a specific field. Historiography also refers to the methods and philosophy of the practice of history.

Marxism: a system of political and economic ideas presented by the German philosopher Karl Marx, notably in his book *Capital*, published as *Das Kapital* in 1867. Marxism centers on the concept of class struggle as a necessary driving force in history and the belief that a revolution by the working class would result in a more just, classless society.

McCarthyism: usually refers to the political climate created by the anti-communist witch-hunts of Republican US Senator McCarthy in the 1950s. During the McCarthy era, thousands of Americans were accused of, and tried and punished for, sympathizing with communist ideas and objectives; some lost their jobs, some were placed on blacklists, and others were imprisoned.

Miscegenation: refers to the mixture of people from different racial groups through marriage, cohabitation, or sexual relations. Despite the prevalence of racism, such relationships existed during and after slavery in the US South. A number of laws in the United States, and in Nazi Germany and apartheid South Africa, forbade miscegenation.

Nazism: the ideological and political position of the German Nazi Party that controlled Germany between 1933 and 1945. A Nazi, or supporter of Nazism, is a fascist and supports militaristic and anti-Semitic (anti-Jewish) ideas and policies.

New Left: a political movement that emerged in the 1960s and campaigned for reform on a broad range of social and cultural issues, such as gay rights, abortion, gender roles, and drug legalization. The

New Left defined itself against the earlier "old" left or Marxist movements that had focused mostly on economic, labor, and class issues.

New Social History: an approach to history that emerged in the 1960s and 1970s and sought to use social scientific analysis as a central analytical tool. It employed, in particular, statistical analyses of large population groups to highlight broad social trends. Influenced by the New Left,* it focused on history "from below" rather than on that directed by elites.

Paternalism: a behavior or attitude designed to limit the autonomy, or independence, of an individual or group, apparently for their good. It is usually associated with a sense of superiority, but also one of care and concern, as of a parent toward a child.

Political correctness: a disparaging term that refers to the moral condemnation of language, actions, or policies thought to be "offensive" to some groups. Critics argue that political correctness places avoidance of offence as a higher priority than freedom of expression and can therefore promote or produce censorship.

Poststructuralist: a critical philosophical approach that is often applied to both social and language systems. It notes the tendency of structuralist thinkers to rely upon binary ways of thinking (e.g. man–woman, capitalist–worker, night–day, city–country) and seeks to deconstruct these binary oppositions.

Precapitalism: the period before the introduction of capitalism, an economic system based on private ownership, private enterprise, and the maximization of profit.

Revisionist: reinterpreting orthodox understandings of a subject.

Vietcong: a slang term for the National Liberation Front of South Vietnam that was the main political and military opposition to the United States in the Vietnam War (1955–75).

Vietnam War (1955–75): a Cold War conflict between the United States and the communist forces of North Vietnam. In 1973, the US signed a peace treaty and withdrew its forces from South Vietnam, which collapsed two years later.

World War II: the global conflict that took place between 1939 and 1945, with Germany, Italy, and Japan (the Axis powers) on one side, and Britain, the Soviet Union, the United States, and other nations (the Allies) on the other.

Zeitgeist: the general ideas, beliefs, and defining spirit or mood of a particular time or place.

PEOPLE MENTIONED IN THE TEXT

James D. Anderson is an American historian of education and race. His book *The Education of Blacks in the South, 1860–1935* won the American Educational Research Association Outstanding Book Award in 1990. He is Edward William and Jane Marr Gutsgell Professor of Education and Professor of History at the University of Illinois at Urbana-Champaign.

Herbert Aptheker (1915–2003) was an American Marxist historian and an outspoken member of the Communist Party USA, which he joined in 1939. In the 1950s, he was blacklisted and denied a college position for over a decade. From 1969, he taught a course on African American history at Bryn Mawr College.

Edward E. Baptist is an American historian of slavery, the US South, and global capitalism. He is associate professor of history at Cornell University and author of *Half Has Never Been Told: Slavery and the Making of American Capitalism* (2014).

Ira Berlin (b. 1941) is an American historian of slavery. He is Distinguished University Professor at the University of Maryland and the author of many books, including *Many Thousands Gone: The First Two Centuries of Slavery in North America* (1998), which won the Bancroft Prize.

John Blassingame (1940–2000) was an American historian of slavery. He was a professor of history and American studies, and chair of the African American Studies program at Yale University. He published several books, including *The Slave Community* (1972).

Charles Dew (b. 1937) is an American historian of the US South and the American Civil War. He is Ephraim Williams Professor of American History at Williams College and the author of three books, including *Apostles of Disunion* (2001).

Stanley Elkins (1925–2013) was an American historian of politics in the early American republic and of slavery in the antebellum South. After teaching at the University of Chicago from 1955 to 1960, he joined the faculty at Smith College in 1960, where he was the Sydenham Clark Parsons Professor of History until his death in 2013.

Elizabeth Fox-Genovese (1941–2007) was a feminist American historian known for her writing about women and society in the antebellum South. She was the founding director of the Institute for Women's Studies at Emory University and is best known for her 1988 book *Within the Plantation Household*.

George M. Frederickson (1934–2008) was an American historian of race and racism and was best known for his work in comparative history. He was Edgar E. Robinson Professor of History at Stanford University.

Michael A. Gomez is an American historian of the African diaspora (the dispersion of African people from their homeland), slavery, and the transatlantic slave trade. From 2000 to 2007 he was director of the Association for the Study of the Worldwide African Diaspora (ASWAD). He is now professor of history and Middle Eastern and Islamic studies at New York University.

Antonio Gramsci (1891–1937) was an Italian Marxist theorist who developed the concept of "cultural hegemony" (or cultural ascendancy) to explain how the ruling class maintain their dominance over others in capitalist society.

Herbert G. Gutman (1928–85) was an American historian of slavery and labor. He was a professor of history at CUNY Graduate Centre and best known for his essays on working-class history and his *The Black Family in Slavery and Freedom, 1750–1925* (1977).

Steven Hahn (b. 1951) is an American historian of the US South, slavery, and popular politics. He is the Roy F. and Jeannette P. Nichols Professor in American History at the University of Pennsylvania.

G. W. F. Hegel (1770–1831) was an influential German idealist philosopher who developed the notion of the master–slave dialectic. He held posts at the Universities of Heidelberg and Berlin.

Charles Joyner is an American historian of slavery and the US South. He is Burroughs Distinguished Professor of Southern History and Culture Emeritus at Coastal Carolina University.

Richard H. King (b. 1942) is an American intellectual historian who writes on questions of race and civil rights in the South. He is professor emeritus at the University of Nottingham and author of *Civil Rights and the Idea of Freedom* (1992) and *Race, Culture and the Intellectuals, 1940–1970* (2004), among others.

Peter Kolchin (b. 1943) is an American historian of slavery and the US South. He is the Henry Clay Reed Professor of History at the University of Delaware.

Christopher Lasch (1932–94) was an American historian, sociologist, and social critic. He was a professor of history at the University of Rochester from 1970 to 1994 and the author of many books, including the classic text *The Culture of Narcissism* (1979).

Lawrence W. Levine (1933–2006) was an American cultural historian who taught at Princeton, the University of California, Berkeley, and George Mason University. He published several works, including the groundbreaking *Black Culture and Black Consciousness: Afro-American Folk Thought from Slavery to Freedom* (1978).

Karl Marx (1818–83) was enormously influential German economist, historian, philosopher, and social theorist whose conception of history and economic writings provided the ideological basis for communism.

James Oakes (b. 1953) is an American historian of slavery and the US South. He is Distinguished Professor of History and Graduate School Humanities Professor at the Graduate Center of the City University of New York.

Ulrich B. Phillips (1877–1934) was an American historian of the US South and of antebellum American slavery. He taught at various institutions, including the University of Wisconsin (1902–6), the University of Michigan (1911–29), and Yale University (1929–34).

James L. Roark is an American historian of slavery and the nineteenth-century US South. He is Samuel Candler Dobbs Professor of American History at Emory University.

Manisha Sinha is an Indian-born historian of American slavery and race relations. She is professor of Afro-American studies and professor of history at the University of Massachusetts-Amherst.

Dianne Miller Sommerville is an American historian of race, gender, and the US South. She is Associate Professor of History at SUNY-Binghamton.

Kenneth M. Stampp (1912–2009) was an American historian of the American Civil War, slavery, and Reconstruction. He held the Alexander F. and May T. Morrison Professorship of History at the University of California, Berkeley from 1946 until 1983.

Edward Palmer "E. P." Thompson (1924–93) was a British historian, writer, socialist, and peace campaigner, as well as a prolific journal and essay writer. He is best known for his historical work on the British radical movements of the late eighteenth and early nineteenth centuries.

Emily West (b. 1971) is a British historian of American slavery and gender. She is Associate Professor of History at Reading University.

Bertram Wyatt-Brown (1932–2012) was an American historian of slavery and the American South. He was Richard J. Milbauer Professor at the University of Florida between 1983 and 2004 and the author of many books on the South, including *Southern Honor* (1982).

WORKS CITED

WORKS CITED

Academic in Exile. "Weighing in on a Heavy-Weight: Genovese's *Roll, Jordan, Roll*." September 3, 2011. https://academicinexile.wordpress. com/2011/09/03/weighing-in-on-a-heavy-weight-genoveses-roll-jordan-roll/.

Alexander Hamilton Institute for the Study of Western Civilization and the Center for African American Studies. "Slavery and Southern History: The Work of Eugene Genovese." Conference, Princeton University, March 25, 2011. http://web.princeton.edu/sites/jmadison/calendar/documents/2011%20 0325%20Genovese%20Brochure%20%282%29.pdf. Conference video: http:// vimeo.com/album/1629546.

Anderson, James D. "Aunt Jemima in Dialectics: Genovese on Slave Culture." *Journal of African American History* 87 (Winter 2002): 26–42.

Aptheker, Herbert. *American Negro Slave Revolts*. New York: International Publishers, 1943; reprint 1974.

Baptist, Edward E. *Half Has Never Been Told: Slavery and the Making of American Capitalism*. New York: Basic Books, 2014.

Berlin, Ira. "Introduction: Herbert G. Gutman and the American Working Class." In Herbert G. Gutman, *Power and Culture: Essays on the American Working Class*. New York: Pantheon Books, 1987.

———. *Many Thousands Gone: The First Two Centuries of Slavery in North America*. Cambridge, MA: Harvard University Press, 1998.

Blassingame, John W. "*Roll, Jordan, Roll: The World the Slaves Made*, by Eugene D. Genovese." *Journal of Social History* 9, no. 3 (Spring 1976): 403–9.

———. *The Slave Community: Plantation Life in the Antebellum South*. New York: Oxford University Press, 1979.

Craton, Michael. *Testing the Chains: Resistance to Slavery in the British West Indies*. Ithaca, NY: Cornell University Press, 2009.

Dew, Charles B. "The Sambo and Nat Turner in Everyslave: A Review of *Roll, Jordan, Roll*." *Civil War History*, 21, no. 3 (September 1975): 261–8.

Elkins, Stanley. *Slavery: A Problem in American Institutional and Intellectual Life*. Chicago: University of Chicago Press, 1959.

Fredrickson, George M. *The Arrogance of Race*. Middletown, CT: Wesleyan University Press, 1989.

———. "*Roll, Jordan, Roll: The World the Slaves Made*, by Eugene D.

Genovese." *Journal of American History* 62, no. 1 (June 1975): 130–3.

Fredrickson, George, and Christopher Lasch. "Resistance to Slavery." *Civil War History* 13 (1967): 316.

Gaspar, David Barry. *Bondmen and Rebels: A Study of Master–Slave Relations in Antigua*. Durham, NC: Duke University Press, 1993.

Genovese, Eugene D. *From Rebellion to Revolution: Afro-American Slave Revolts in the Making of the Modern World*. Baton Rouge: Louisiana State University Press, 1979.

———. *In Red and Black: Marxian Explorations in Southern and Afro-American History*. New York: Vintage Books, 1971.

———. *The Political Economy of Slavery: Studies in the Economy and Society of the Slave South*. New York: Vintage Books, 1965.

———. "A Reply to Criticism." *Radical History Review* 13 (1977): 94–114.

———. *Roll, Jordan, Roll: The World the Slaves Made*. New York: Vintage Books, 1976.

———. *The World the Slaveholders Made: Two Essays in Interpretation*. New York: Vintage Books, 1969.

———. *Fatal Self-Deception: Slaveholding Paternalism in the Old South*. Cambridge: Cambridge University Press, 2011.

———. *Fruits of Merchant Capital: Slavery and Bourgeois Property in the Rise and Expansion of Capitalism*. Oxford: Oxford University Press, 1983.

———. *The Mind of the Master Class: History and Faith in the Southern Slaveholders' Worldview*. New York: Cambridge University Press, 2005.

Gomez, Michael A. *Exchanging Our Country Marks: The Transformation of African Identities in the Colonial and Antebellum South*. Chapel Hill: University of North Carolina Press, 1998.

Gottfried, Paul. "Eugene D. Genovese, R.I.P." September 27, 2012. *The American Conservative*.

Gutman, Herbert G. *The Black Family in Slavery and Freedom*. New York: Vintage Books, 1977.

Hahn, Steven. "From Radical to Right-Wing: The Legacy of Eugene Genovese." *The New Republic*, October 2, 2012. Accessed June 30, 2015. http://www.newrepublic.com/article/books-and-arts/108044/radical-right-wing-the-legacy-eugene-genovese.

Joyner, Charles. *Down by the Riverside: A South Carolina Slave Community*. Champaign: University of Illinois Press, 1985.

King, Richard H. "Marxism and the Slave South." Review of *The Political Economy of Slavery* by Eugene Genovese; *The World the Slaveholders Made* by Eugene Genovese; *In Red and Black: Marxian Explorations in Southern and Afro-American History* by Eugene Genovese; *Roll, Jordan, Roll* by Eugene Genovese. *American Quarterly* 29, no. 1 (Spring 1977): 117–31.

Kolchin, Peter. "Eugene D. Genovese: Historian of Slavery." *Radical History Review* 88 (Winter 2004): 52–67.

— — —. "*Fatal Self-Deception: Slaveholding Paternalism in the Old South,* by Eugene D. Genovese and Elizabeth Fox-Genovese," *Civil War History* 59, no. 2 (June 2013): 242–3. Accessed August 11, 2015. http://muse. jhu.edu/login?auth=0&type=summary&url=/journals/civil_war_history/ v059/59.2.kolchin.html.

Kolchin, Peter et al. "Genovese Forum." *Radical History Review* 88 (Winter 2004).

Lichtenstein, Alex. "Right Church, Wrong Pew: Eugene Genovese and Southern Conservatism." *New Politics*, 6(3), no. 23 (Summer 1997). Accessed August 6, 2015. http://nova.wpunj.edu/newpolitics/issue23/lichte23.htm.

Martin, Douglas. "Eugene D. Genovese, Historian of South, Dies at 82." *New York Times,* September 29, 2012. Accessed June 25, 2015. http://www. nytimes.com/2012/09/30/us/eugene-d-genovese-historian-of-south-dies-at-82. html?_r=0.

Nash, Gary. "Think Tank; A Rebellion Against History's Fuzzy Future." *New York Times*, May 2, 1998. Accessed June 30, 2015. http://www.nytimes. com/1998/05/02/arts/think-tank-a-rebellion-against-history-s-fuzzy-future.html.

Novick, Peter. *That Noble Dream: The "Objectivity Question" and the American Historical Profession*. Cambridge: Cambridge University Press, 1988.

Oakes, James. *The Ruling Race: A History of American Slaveholders* (London: W. W. Norton, 1998).

Phillips, Ulrich B. *American Negro Slavery*. New York: D. Appleton & Co., 1918.

— — —. *American Negro Slavery: A Survey of the Supply, Employment and Control of Negro Labor as Determined by the Plantation Regime*. Baton Rouge: Louisiana State University Press, 1966 [new edition, with a new foreword]).

— — —. "The Central Theme of Southern History." *American Historical Review* 34, no. 1 (1928): 30–43.

— — —. *Life and Labor in the Old South*. Boston: Little Brown & Co., 1929.

Roark, James L. "*The Ruling Race: A History of American Slaveholders* by James Oakes." *American Historical Review* 88, no. 4 (October 1983): 1067.

Sinha, Manisha. "Eugene D. Genovese: The Mind of a Marxist Conservative." *Radical History Review* 88 (Winter 2004): 4–29.

Smith, John David. "The Life and Labor of Ulrich Bonnell Phillips." *Georgia Historical Quarterly* 70, no. 2 (Summer 1986): 254–72.

Sommerville, Dianne Miller. "Moonlight, Magnolias, and Brigadoon; or, 'Almost Like Being in Love': Mastery and Sexual Exploitation in Eugene D. Genovese's Plantation South." *Radical History Review* 88, no. 4 (2004): 68–82.

Stampp, Kenneth. *The Peculiar Institution: Slavery in the Antebellum South*. New York: Knopf, 1956.

Thompson, E. P. *The Making of the English Working Class*. London: Victor Gollancz, 1963.

West, Emily. *Enslaved Women in America: From Colonial Times to Emancipation*. Lanham, MD: Rowman & Littlefield, 2014.

Womack, John, Lou Ferlerger, and Robert Paquette. "Roll, Jordan, Roll." *New York Review of Books*, November 24, 1998. Accessed August 6, 2014. http://www.nybooks.com/articles/archives/1988/nov/24/roll-jordan-roll/.

Woo, Elaine. "Eugene Genovese Dies at 82; Leftist Historian Turned Conservative." *Los Angeles Times*, October 15, 2012. Accessed June 29, 2015. http://articles.latimes.com/2012/oct/15/local/la-me-eugene-genovese-20121015

Wyatt-Brown, Bertram. "*Roll, Jordan, Roll: The World the Slaves Made*, by Eugene D. Genovese." *Journal of Southern History* 41, no. 2 (May 1975): 240–2.

THE MACAT LIBRARY
BY DISCIPLINE

The Macat Library By Discipline

AFRICANA STUDIES

Chinua Achebe's *An Image of Africa: Racism in Conrad's Heart of Darkness*
W. E. B. Du Bois's *The Souls of Black Folk*
Zora Neale Huston's *Characteristics of Negro Expression*
Martin Luther King Jr's *Why We Can't Wait*
Toni Morrison's *Playing in the Dark: Whiteness in the American Literary Imagination*

ANTHROPOLOGY

Arjun Appadurai's *Modernity at Large: Cultural Dimensions of Globalisation*
Philippe Ariès's *Centuries of Childhood*
Franz Boas's *Race, Language and Culture*
Kim Chan & Renée Mauborgne's *Blue Ocean Strategy*
Jared Diamond's *Guns, Germs & Steel: the Fate of Human Societies*
Jared Diamond's *Collapse: How Societies Choose to Fail or Survive*
E. E. Evans-Pritchard's *Witchcraft, Oracles and Magic Among the Azande*
James Ferguson's *The Anti-Politics Machine*
Clifford Geertz's *The Interpretation of Cultures*
David Graeber's *Debt: the First 5000 Years*
Karen Ho's *Liquidated: An Ethnography of Wall Street*
Geert Hofstede's *Culture's Consequences: Comparing Values, Behaviors, Institutes and Organizations across Nations*
Claude Lévi-Strauss's *Structural Anthropology*
Jay Macleod's *Ain't No Makin' It: Aspirations and Attainment in a Low-Income Neighborhood*
Saba Mahmood's *The Politics of Piety: The Islamic Revival and the Feminist Subjec*t
Marcel Mauss's *The Gift*

BUSINESS

Jean Lave & Etienne Wenger's *Situated Learning*
Theodore Levitt's *Marketing Myopia*
Burton G. Malkiel's *A Random Walk Down Wall Street*
Douglas McGregor's *The Human Side of Enterprise*
Michael Porter's *Competitive Strategy: Creating and Sustaining Superior Performance*
John Kotter's *Leading Change*
C. K. Prahalad & Gary Hamel's *The Core Competence of the Corporation*

CRIMINOLOGY

Michelle Alexander's *The New Jim Crow: Mass Incarceration in the Age of Colorblindness*
Michael R. Gottfredson & Travis Hirschi's *A General Theory of Crime*
Richard Herrnstein & Charles A. Murray's *The Bell Curve: Intelligence and Class Structure in American Life*
Elizabeth Loftus's *Eyewitness Testimony*
Jay Macleod's *Ain't No Makin' It: Aspirations and Attainment in a Low-Income Neighborhood*
Philip Zimbardo's *The Lucifer Effect*

ECONOMICS

Janet Abu-Lughod's *Before European Hegemony*
Ha-Joon Chang's *Kicking Away the Ladder*
David Brion Davis's *The Problem of Slavery in the Age of Revolution*
Milton Friedman's *The Role of Monetary Policy*
Milton Friedman's *Capitalism and Freedom*
David Graeber's *Debt: the First 5000 Years*
Friedrich Hayek's *The Road to Serfdom*
Karen Ho's *Liquidated: An Ethnography of Wall Street*

The Macat Library By Discipline

John Maynard Keynes's *The General Theory of Employment, Interest and Money*
Charles P. Kindleberger's *Manias, Panics and Crashes*
Robert Lucas's *Why Doesn't Capital Flow from Rich to Poor Countries?*
Burton G. Malkiel's *A Random Walk Down Wall Street*
Thomas Robert Malthus's *An Essay on the Principle of Population*
Karl Marx's *Capital*
Thomas Piketty's *Capital in the Twenty-First Century*
Amartya Sen's *Development as Freedom*
Adam Smith's *The Wealth of Nations*
Nassim Nicholas Taleb's *The Black Swan: The Impact of the Highly Improbable*
Amos Tversky's & Daniel Kahneman's *Judgment under Uncertainty: Heuristics and Biases*
Mahbub Ul Haq's *Reflections on Human Development*
Max Weber's *The Protestant Ethic and the Spirit of Capitalism*

FEMINISM AND GENDER STUDIES

Judith Butler's *Gender Trouble*
Simone De Beauvoir's *The Second Sex*
Michel Foucault's *History of Sexuality*
Betty Friedan's *The Feminine Mystique*
Saba Mahmood's *The Politics of Piety: The Islamic Revival and the Feminist Subject*
Joan Wallach Scott's *Gender and the Politics of History*
Mary Wollstonecraft's *A Vindication of the Rights of Woman*
Virginia Woolf's *A Room of One's Own*

GEOGRAPHY

The Brundtland Report's *Our Common Future*
Rachel Carson's *Silent Spring*
Charles Darwin's *On the Origin of Species*
James Ferguson's *The Anti-Politics Machine*
Jane Jacobs's *The Death and Life of Great American Cities*
James Lovelock's *Gaia: A New Look at Life on Earth*
Amartya Sen's *Development as Freedom*
Mathis Wackernagel & William Rees's *Our Ecological Footprint*

HISTORY

Janet Abu-Lughod's *Before European Hegemony*
Benedict Anderson's *Imagined Communities*
Bernard Bailyn's *The Ideological Origins of the American Revolution*
Hanna Batatu's *The Old Social Classes And The Revolutionary Movements Of Iraq*
Christopher Browning's *Ordinary Men: Reserve Police Batallion 101 and the Final Solution in Poland*
Edmund Burke's *Reflections on the Revolution in France*
William Cronon's *Nature's Metropolis: Chicago And The Great West*
Alfred W. Crosby's *The Columbian Exchange*
Hamid Dabashi's *Iran: A People Interrupted*
David Brion Davis's *The Problem of Slavery in the Age of Revolution*
Nathalie Zemon Davis's *The Return of Martin Guerre*
Jared Diamond's *Guns, Germs & Steel: the Fate of Human Societies*
Frank Dikotter's *Mao's Great Famine*
John W Dower's *War Without Mercy: Race And Power In The Pacific War*
W. E. B. Du Bois's *The Souls of Black Folk*
Richard J. Evans's *In Defence of History*
Lucien Febvre's *The Problem of Unbelief in the 16th Century*
Sheila Fitzpatrick's *Everyday Stalinism*

Eric Foner's *Reconstruction: America's Unfinished Revolution, 1863-1877*
Michel Foucault's *Discipline and Punish*
Michel Foucault's *History of Sexuality*
Francis Fukuyama's *The End of History and the Last Man*
John Lewis Gaddis's *We Now Know: Rethinking Cold War History*
Ernest Gellner's *Nations and Nationalism*
Eugene Genovese's *Roll, Jordan, Roll: The World the Slaves Made*
Carlo Ginzburg's *The Night Battles*
Daniel Goldhagen's *Hitler's Willing Executioners*
Jack Goldstone's *Revolution and Rebellion in the Early Modern World*
Antonio Gramsci's *The Prison Notebooks*
Alexander Hamilton, John Jay & James Madison's *The Federalist Papers*
Christopher Hill's *The World Turned Upside Down*
Carole Hillenbrand's *The Crusades: Islamic Perspectives*
Thomas Hobbes's *Leviathan*
Eric Hobsbawm's *The Age Of Revolution*
John A. Hobson's *Imperialism: A Study*
Albert Hourani's *History of the Arab Peoples*
Samuel P. Huntington's *The Clash of Civilizations and the Remaking of World Order*
C. L. R. James's *The Black Jacobins*
Tony Judt's *Postwar: A History of Europe Since 1945*
Ernst Kantorowicz's *The King's Two Bodies: A Study in Medieval Political Theology*
Paul Kennedy's *The Rise and Fall of the Great Powers*
Ian Kershaw's *The "Hitler Myth": Image and Reality in the Third Reich*
John Maynard Keynes's *The General Theory of Employment, Interest and Money*
Charles P. Kindleberger's *Manias, Panics and Crashes*
Martin Luther King Jr's *Why We Can't Wait*
Henry Kissinger's *World Order: Reflections on the Character of Nations and the Course of History*
Thomas Kuhn's *The Structure of Scientific Revolutions*
Georges Lefebvre's *The Coming of the French Revolution*
John Locke's *Two Treatises of Government*
Niccolò Machiavelli's *The Prince*
Thomas Robert Malthus's *An Essay on the Principle of Population*
Mahmood Mamdani's *Citizen and Subject: Contemporary Africa And The Legacy Of Late Colonialism*
Karl Marx's *Capital*
Stanley Milgram's *Obedience to Authority*
John Stuart Mill's *On Liberty*
Thomas Paine's *Common Sense*
Thomas Paine's *Rights of Man*
Geoffrey Parker's *Global Crisis: War, Climate Change and Catastrophe in the Seventeenth Century*
Jonathan Riley-Smith's *The First Crusade and the Idea of Crusading*
Jean-Jacques Rousseau's *The Social Contract*
Joan Wallach Scott's *Gender and the Politics of History*
Theda Skocpol's *States and Social Revolutions*
Adam Smith's *The Wealth of Nations*
Timothy Snyder's *Bloodlands: Europe Between Hitler and Stalin*
Sun Tzu's *The Art of War*
Keith Thomas's *Religion and the Decline of Magic*
Thucydides's *The History of the Peloponnesian War*
Frederick Jackson Turner's *The Significance of the Frontier in American History*
Odd Arne Westad's *The Global Cold War: Third World Interventions And The Making Of Our Times*

The Macat Library By Discipline

LITERATURE

Chinua Achebe's *An Image of Africa: Racism in Conrad's Heart of Darkness*
Roland Barthes's *Mythologies*
Homi K. Bhabha's *The Location of Culture*
Judith Butler's *Gender Trouble*
Simone De Beauvoir's *The Second Sex*
Ferdinand De Saussure's *Course in General Linguistics*
T. S. Eliot's *The Sacred Wood: Essays on Poetry and Criticism*
Zora Neale Huston's *Characteristics of Negro Expression*
Toni Morrison's *Playing in the Dark: Whiteness in the American Literary Imagination*
Edward Said's *Orientalism*
Gayatri Chakravorty Spivak's *Can the Subaltern Speak?*
Mary Wollstonecraft's *A Vindication of the Rights of Women*
Virginia Woolf's *A Room of One's Own*

PHILOSOPHY

Elizabeth Anscombe's *Modern Moral Philosophy*
Hannah Arendt's *The Human Condition*
Aristotle's *Metaphysics*
Aristotle's *Nicomachean Ethics*
Edmund Gettier's *Is Justified True Belief Knowledge?*
Georg Wilhelm Friedrich Hegel's *Phenomenology of Spirit*
David Hume's *Dialogues Concerning Natural Religion*
David Hume's *The Enquiry for Human Understanding*
Immanuel Kant's *Religion within the Boundaries of Mere Reason*
Immanuel Kant's *Critique of Pure Reason*
Søren Kierkegaard's *The Sickness Unto Death*
Søren Kierkegaard's *Fear and Trembling*
C. S. Lewis's *The Abolition of Man*
Alasdair MacIntyre's *After Virtue*
Marcus Aurelius's *Meditations*
Friedrich Nietzsche's *On the Genealogy of Morality*
Friedrich Nietzsche's *Beyond Good and Evil*
Plato's *Republic*
Plato's *Symposium*
Jean-Jacques Rousseau's *The Social Contract*
Gilbert Ryle's *The Concept of Mind*
Baruch Spinoza's *Ethics*
Sun Tzu's *The Art of War*
Ludwig Wittgenstein's *Philosophical Investigations*

POLITICS

Benedict Anderson's *Imagined Communities*
Aristotle's *Politics*
Bernard Bailyn's *The Ideological Origins of the American Revolution*
Edmund Burke's *Reflections on the Revolution in France*
John C. Calhoun's *A Disquisition on Government*
Ha-Joon Chang's *Kicking Away the Ladder*
Hamid Dabashi's *Iran: A People Interrupted*
Hamid Dabashi's *Theology of Discontent: The Ideological Foundation of the Islamic Revolution in Iran*
Robert Dahl's *Democracy and its Critics*
Robert Dahl's *Who Governs?*
David Brion Davis's *The Problem of Slavery in the Age of Revolution*

Alexis De Tocqueville's *Democracy in America*
James Ferguson's *The Anti-Politics Machine*
Frank Dikotter's *Mao's Great Famine*
Sheila Fitzpatrick's *Everyday Stalinism*
Eric Foner's *Reconstruction: America's Unfinished Revolution, 1863-1877*
Milton Friedman's *Capitalism and Freedom*
Francis Fukuyama's *The End of History and the Last Man*
John Lewis Gaddis's *We Now Know: Rethinking Cold War History*
Ernest Gellner's *Nations and Nationalism*
David Graeber's *Debt: the First 5000 Years*
Antonio Gramsci's *The Prison Notebooks*
Alexander Hamilton, John Jay & James Madison's *The Federalist Papers*
Friedrich Hayek's *The Road to Serfdom*
Christopher Hill's *The World Turned Upside Down*
Thomas Hobbes's *Leviathan*
John A. Hobson's *Imperialism: A Study*
Samuel P. Huntington's *The Clash of Civilizations and the Remaking of World Order*
Tony Judt's *Postwar: A History of Europe Since 1945*
David C. Kang's *China Rising: Peace, Power and Order in East Asia*
Paul Kennedy's *The Rise and Fall of Great Powers*
Robert Keohane's *After Hegemony*
Martin Luther King Jr.'s *Why We Can't Wait*
Henry Kissinger's *World Order: Reflections on the Character of Nations and the Course of History*
John Locke's *Two Treatises of Government*
Niccolò Machiavelli's *The Prince*
Thomas Robert Malthus's *An Essay on the Principle of Population*
Mahmood Mamdani's *Citizen and Subject: Contemporary Africa And The Legacy Of Late Colonialism*
Karl Marx's *Capital*
John Stuart Mill's *On Liberty*
John Stuart Mill's *Utilitarianism*
Hans Morgenthau's *Politics Among Nations*
Thomas Paine's *Common Sense*
Thomas Paine's *Rights of Man*
Thomas Piketty's *Capital in the Twenty-First Century*
Robert D. Putman's *Bowling Alone*
John Rawls's *Theory of Justice*
Jean-Jacques Rousseau's *The Social Contract*
Theda Skocpol's *States and Social Revolutions*
Adam Smith's *The Wealth of Nations*
Sun Tzu's *The Art of War*
Henry David Thoreau's *Civil Disobedience*
Thucydides's *The History of the Peloponnesian War*
Kenneth Waltz's *Theory of International Politics*
Max Weber's *Politics as a Vocation*
Odd Arne Westad's *The Global Cold War: Third World Interventions And The Making Of Our Times*

POSTCOLONIAL STUDIES

Roland Barthes's *Mythologies*
Frantz Fanon's *Black Skin, White Masks*
Homi K. Bhabha's *The Location of Culture*
Gustavo Gutiérrez's *A Theology of Liberation*
Edward Said's *Orientalism*
Gayatri Chakravorty Spivak's *Can the Subaltern Speak?*

The Macat Library By Discipline

Thomas Piketty's *Capital in the Twenty-First Century*
Robert D. Putman's *Bowling Alone*
David Riesman's *The Lonely Crowd: A Study of the Changing American Character*
Edward Said's *Orientalism*
Joan Wallach Scott's *Gender and the Politics of History*
Theda Skocpol's *States and Social Revolutions*
Max Weber's *The Protestant Ethic and the Spirit of Capitalism*

THEOLOGY

Augustine's *Confessions*
Benedict's *Rule of St Benedict*
Gustavo Gutiérrez's *A Theology of Liberation*
Carole Hillenbrand's *The Crusades: Islamic Perspectives*
David Hume's *Dialogues Concerning Natural Religion*
Immanuel Kant's *Religion within the Boundaries of Mere Reason*
Ernst Kantorowicz's *The King's Two Bodies: A Study in Medieval Political Theology*
Søren Kierkegaard's *The Sickness Unto Death*
C. S. Lewis's *The Abolition of Man*
Saba Mahmood's *The Politics of Piety: The Islamic Revival and the Feminist Subject*
Baruch Spinoza's *Ethics*
Keith Thomas's *Religion and the Decline of Magic*

COMING SOON

Chris Argyris's *The Individual and the Organisation*
Seyla Benhabib's *The Rights of Others*
Walter Benjamin's *The Work Of Art in the Age of Mechanical Reproduction*
John Berger's *Ways of Seeing*
Pierre Bourdieu's *Outline of a Theory of Practice*
Mary Douglas's *Purity and Danger*
Roland Dworkin's *Taking Rights Seriously*
James G. March's *Exploration and Exploitation in Organisational Learning*
Ikujiro Nonaka's *A Dynamic Theory of Organizational Knowledge Creation*
Griselda Pollock's *Vision and Difference*
Amartya Sen's *Inequality Re-Examined*
Susan Sontag's *On Photography*
Yasser Tabbaa's *The Transformation of Islamic Art*
Ludwig von Mises's *Theory of Money and Credit*

Macat Disciplines

Access the greatest ideas and thinkers across entire disciplines, including

AFRICANA STUDIES

Chinua Achebe's *An Image of Africa: Racism in Conrad's Heart of Darkness*

W. E. B. Du Bois's *The Souls of Black Folk*

Zora Neale Hurston's *Characteristics of Negro Expression*

Martin Luther King Jr.'s *Why We Can't Wait*

Toni Morrison's *Playing in the Dark: Whiteness in the American Literary Imagination*

Macat analyses are available from all good bookshops and libraries.

Access hundreds of analyses through one, multimedia tool.

Macat Disciplines

*Access the greatest ideas and thinkers
across entire disciplines, including*

FEMINISM, GENDER AND QUEER STUDIES

Simone De Beauvoir's
The Second Sex

Michel Foucault's
History of Sexuality

Betty Friedan's
The Feminine Mystique

Saba Mahmood's
*The Politics of Piety:
The Islamic Revival and
the Feminist Subject*

Joan Wallach Scott's
*Gender and the
Politics of History*

Mary Wollstonecraft's
*A Vindication of the
Rights of Woman*

Virginia Woolf's
A Room of One's Own

Judith Butler's
Gender Trouble

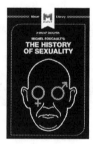

Macat analyses are available from all good bookshops and libraries.

Access hundreds of analyses through one, multimedia tool.

Join free for one month library.macat.com

Macat Disciplines

Access the greatest ideas and thinkers across entire disciplines, including

INEQUALITY

Ha-Joon Chang's, *Kicking Away the Ladder*

David Graeber's, *Debt: The First 5000 Years*

Robert E. Lucas's, *Why Doesn't Capital Flow from Rich To Poor Countries?*

Thomas Piketty's, *Capital in the Twenty-First Century*

Amartya Sen's, *Inequality Re-Examined*

Mahbub Ul Haq's, *Reflections on Human Development*

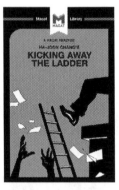

Macat analyses are available from all good bookshops and libraries.

Access hundreds of analyses through one, multimedia tool.

Join free for one month **libra** **macat.com**

Macat Disciplines

Access the greatest ideas and thinkers across entire disciplines, including

CRIMINOLOGY

Michelle Alexander's
The New Jim Crow: Mass Incarceration in the Age of Colorblindness

Michael R. Gottfredson & Travis Hirschi's
A General Theory of Crime

Elizabeth Loftus's
Eyewitness Testimony

Richard Herrnstein & Charles A. Murray's
The Bell Curve: Intelligence and Class Structure in American Life

Jay Macleod's
Ain't No Makin' It: Aspirations and Attainment in a Low-Income Neighborhood

Philip Zimbardo's
The Lucifer Effect

Macat analyses are available from all good bookshops and libraries.

Access hundreds of analyses through one, multimedia tool.

Macat Disciplines

Access the greatest ideas and thinkers across entire disciplines, including

Postcolonial Studies

Roland Barthes's *Mythologies*
Frantz Fanon's *Black Skin, White Masks*
Homi K. Bhabha's *The Location of Culture*
Gustavo Gutiérrez's *A Theology of Liberation*
Edward Said's *Orientalism*
Gayatri Chakravorty Spivak's *Can the Subaltern Speak?*

Macat analyses are available from all good bookshops and libraries.

Access hundreds of analyses through one, multimedia tool.

Join free for one month **library.macat.com**

Macat Disciplines

Access the greatest ideas and thinkers across entire disciplines, including

GLOBALIZATION

Arjun Appadurai's, *Modernity at Large: Cultural Dimensions of Globalisation*

James Ferguson's, *The Anti-Politics Machine*

Geert Hofstede's, *Culture's Consequences*

Amartya Sen's, *Development as Freedom*

Macat analyses are available from all good bookshops and libraries.

Access hundreds of analyses through one, multimedia tool.

Macat Pairs

*Analyse historical and modern issues
from opposite sides of an argument.
Pairs include:*

HOW TO RUN AN ECONOMY

John Maynard Keynes's
The General Theory OF Employment, Interest and Money

Classical economics suggests that market economies are self-correcting in times of recession or depression, and tend toward full employment and output. But English economist John Maynard Keynes disagrees.

In his ground-breaking 1936 study *The General Theory*, Keynes argues that traditional economics has misunderstood the causes of unemployment. Employment is not determined by the price of labor; it is directly linked to demand. Keynes believes market economies are by nature unstable, and so require government intervention. Spurred on by the social catastrophe of the Great Depression of the 1930s, he sets out to revolutionize the way the world thinks

Milton Friedman's
The Role of Monetary Policy

Friedman's 1968 paper changed the course of economic theory. In just 17 pages, he demolished existing theory and outlined an effective alternate monetary policy designed to secure 'high employment, stable prices and rapid growth.'

Friedman demonstrated that monetary policy plays a vital role in broader economic stability and argued that economists got their monetary policy wrong in the 1950s and 1960s by misunderstanding the relationship between inflation and unemployment. Previous generations of economists had believed that governments could permanently decrease unemployment by permitting inflation—and vice versa. Friedman's most original contribution was to show that this supposed trade-off is an illusion that only works in the short term.

Macat analyses are available from all good bookshops and libraries.

Access hundreds of analyses through one, multimedia tool.
Join free for one month **library.macat.com**

Macat Disciplines

Access the greatest ideas and thinkers across entire disciplines, including

TOTALITARIANISM

Sheila Fitzpatrick's, *Everyday Stalinism*
Ian Kershaw's, *The "Hitler Myth"*
Timothy Snyder's, *Bloodlands*

Macat analyses are available from all good bookshops and libraries.

Access hundreds of analyses through one, multimedia tool.

Join free for one month **library.macat.com**

Macat Pairs

Analyse historical and modern issues from opposite sides of an argument. Pairs include:

RACE AND IDENTITY

Zora Neale Hurston's
Characteristics of Negro Expression

Using material collected on anthropological expeditions to the South, Zora Neale Hurston explains how expression in African American culture in the early twentieth century departs from the art of white America. At the time, African American art was often criticized for copying white culture. For Hurston, this criticism misunderstood how art works. European tradition views art as something fixed. But Hurston describes a creative process that is alive, ever-changing, and largely improvisational. She maintains that African American art works through a process called 'mimicry'—where an imitated object or verbal pattern, for example, is reshaped and altered until it becomes something new, novel—and worthy of attention.

Frantz Fanon's
Black Skin, White Masks

Black Skin, White Masks offers a radical analysis of the psychological effects of colonization on the colonized.

Fanon witnessed the effects of colonization first hand both in his birthplace, Martinique, and again later in life when he worked as a psychiatrist in another French colony, Algeria. His text is uncompromising in form and argument. He dissects the dehumanizing effects of colonialism, arguing that it destroys the native sense of identity, forcing people to adapt to an alien set of values—including a core belief that they are inferior. This results in deep psychological trauma.

Fanon's work played a pivotal role in the civil rights movements of the 1960s.

Macat analyses are available from all good bookshops and libraries.

Access hundreds of analyses through one, multimedia tool.
Join free for one month **library.macat.com**

Macat Pairs

Analyse historical and modern issues from opposite sides of an argument. Pairs include:

INTERNATIONAL RELATIONS IN THE 21ST CENTURY

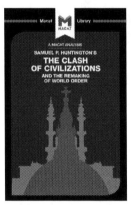

Samuel P. Huntington's
The Clash of Civilisations

In his highly influential 1996 book, Huntington offers a vision of a post-Cold War world in which conflict takes place not between competing ideologies but between cultures. The worst clash, he argues, will be between the Islamic world and the West: the West's arrogance and belief that its culture is a "gift" to the world will come into conflict with Islam's obstinacy and concern that its culture is under attack from a morally decadent "other."

Clash inspired much debate between different political schools of thought. But its greatest impact came in helping define American foreign policy in the wake of the 2001 terrorist attacks in New York and Washington.

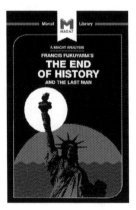

Francis Fukuyama's
The End of History and the Last Man

Published in 1992, *The End of History and the Last Man* argues that capitalist democracy is the final destination for all societies. Fukuyama believed democracy triumphed during the Cold War because it lacks the "fundamental contradictions" inherent in communism and satisfies our yearning for freedom and equality. Democracy therefore marks the endpoint in the evolution of ideology, and so the "end of history." There will still be "events," but no fundamental change in ideology.

Printed in the United States
by Baker & Taylor Publisher Services